W9-ABC-954

Taking Stock
The North American Livestock Census

Donald E. Bixby, Carolyn J. Christman,
Cynthia J. Ehrman and D. Phillip Sponenberg

The American Livestock Breeds Conservancy

The McDonald & Woodward Publishing Company
Blacksburg, Virginia
1994

The McDonald & Woodward Publishing Company
P. O. Box 10308, Blacksburg, Virginia 24062-0308

Taking Stock: The North American Livestock Census
© 1994 by The American Livestock Breeds Conservancy

10 9 8 7 6 5 4 3 2 1

First printing February 1994

Library of Congress Cataloging-in-Publication Data

Taking stock : the North American livestock census / Donald E. Bixby
 ... [et al.] (The American Livestock Breeds Conservancy)
        p.   cm.
   Includes bibliographical references and index.
   ISBN 0-939923-35-1 : $14.95
   1. Livestock—United States—Germplasm resources. 2. Livestock—
Canada—Germplasm resources. 3. Livestock breeds—United
States. 4. Livestock breeds—Canada. I. Bixby, Donald E., 1940–
II. American Livestock Breeds Conservancy.
SF 105.3.T34   1994
636.08'21—dc20   93-47249
                                                   CIP

Rsf

Contents

iii

.

Acknowledgements

This research was supported by grants from CS Fund, Rare Breeds Survival Foundation of America, and the Ruth Mott Fund; gifts from the members of the American Livestock Breeds Conservancy; and USDA contract number 59-0500-2-190. Marleen Felius created the breed illustrations appearing on pages 31, 37, 55, 65, 81, and 95.
Cover: Edward Hicks, *The Cornell Farm*, 1848, courtesy of The National Gallery of Art, Washington, DC.

Preface

The American Livestock Breeds Conservancy

The American Livestock Breeds Conservancy (ALBC) is a non-profit organization working to protect genetic diversity in American livestock through the conservation of nearly 100 breeds of asses, cattle, goats, horses, sheep, swine, and poultry. The organization is supported by gifts from individuals, grants from foundations and corporations, and contracts.

The American Livestock Breeds Conservancy was founded as the American Minor Breeds Conservancy in 1977 in New England. Agricultural historians, while seeking authentic period livestock for interpretive programs at Old Sturbridge Village and other historic sites, discovered that many heritage breeds were nearly extinct. The historians joined with farmers and animal scientists to form AMBC, and set its mission as the conservation of endangered breeds of livestock. The organization moved to Pittsboro, North Carolina in 1985. The name was changed to the American Livestock Breeds Conservancy in 1993 to reflect the increasingly serious threat to all livestock breeds, and a consequent widening of the organization's sphere of activities.

The American Livestock Breeds Conservancy directs many conservation and research programs. A periodic census of livestock breeds, which includes the monitoring of bloodlines within many of the rarer breeds, provides the knowledge base for developing these programs. Conservation projects include a gene bank, blood typing and DNA fingerprinting to characterize breed identity, rescues of threatened populations, and the development of genetic recovery breeding programs. ALBC provides technical support for conservation breeding, registry operation, and livestock use to breeders, breed associations, and agriculture organizations. Outreach programs educate the public and policy makers about the importance of genetic diversity in livestock.

The American Livestock Breeds Conservancy is the national leader in livestock conservation and the clearinghouse for information on endangered breeds of livestock. ALBC is also a founding member of Rare Breeds International, a global network of livestock conservation organizations. For more information about the American Livestock Breeds Conservancy and Livestock Genetic Conservation, write to ALBC, PO Box 477, Pittsboro NC 27312-0477, USA.

Section I

The Conservation of Genetic Diversity in Livestock

Chapter 1

The Importance of Livestock

For over 10,000 years, domesticated animals have been essential to human society and efforts in agriculture. Domesticated species fill a wide array of human needs, including draft power, fiber, food, land management, protection, and transportation. While domesticated species around the world range from guinea pigs to camels, the traditional livestock species of North America are asses, cattle, goats, horses, sheep, and swine. This book examines the current status of these species. The poultry species, due to the differences in the ways they are maintained and documented, are not included here but will be the subject of a future census.

Livestock have always been integral to farming, and they are essential to current efforts to diversify agriculture. The uses of livestock can be roughly divided into animal products and animal services.

The best known animal product is food. The livestock species produce a significant part of our food supply, specifically meat, milk, and cheese. The creation of food from forage is agriculturally significant, as livestock can transform forage nutrients unavailable to humans into foods of high quality for human consumption. Livestock can be raised in regions that are poorly suited to field crops and therefore do not need to compete with plant production for human foods. Instead, livestock can be used as a complement and adjunct to food crop production. Further, well managed livestock production systems have a clearly positive environmental impact by reducing erosion, increasing plant diversity, and protecting grasslands from invasion by woody scrub growth.

High quality natural fibers, such as wool, cashmere, and mohair, are produced by livestock. These natural fibers continue to be in demand since they have qualities unequaled by any synthetic fiber. Leather is another important animal product used for clothing, furniture, book binding, and sporting equipment.

Manure, though actually an animal by-product rather than product, is the most widely used fertilizer in the world. Manure provides essential elements of fertility to the soil and it surpasses the potential of "green" or non-animal composts. Another advantage is that since animals are mobile, they can be moved around a farm to deposit the manure where it is needed.

Animal services — such as grazing, brush clearing, power, and pest control — are less well known to the current agricultural generation (even less to the general public) and therefore merit additional discussion. These services are often the only practical complement or alternative to the use of chemicals, fossil fuels, and machinery in agricultural systems.

Grazing is the feeding on grasses and other non-woody plants. Grazing has recently acquired a bad name with environmentalists due to confusion with overgrazing. Overgrazing can rapidly degrade natural resources, while well-managed grazing can greatly enhance grassland environments. Grasses and other types of forages are part of a biological system that developed under the pressure of grazing and must be grazed in order to be sustained. Most wild grazers are now extinct or greatly reduced in number, so that grazing of livestock has now become a necessary tool to maintain the species diversity of natural grasslands. Furthermore, productive grasslands are an essential part of sound soil management throughout much of North America.

Managed forage production is an excellent method for healing and recovering damaged land. Much of the marginal farmland now in use should in fact be taken out of row crop production and put into permanent or semipermanent forage crops. This would reduce water runoff, erosion by wind and water, and allow for the reestablishment of organic material within the soil. Controlled grazing by livestock is the one sure means to make these marginal regions productive, in both an environmental and economic sense.

Goats, sheep, and some breeds of cattle are particularly good at browsing, that is, consuming saplings, shrubs and other woody plants. Browsing animals can be used to eat rapidly growing pest plants such as leafy spurge, blackberry, kudzu, poison ivy, and many other tenacious invaders. Reduction of these pest plants allows for the recovery of natural diversity and also for the long term establishment of productive natural forage systems.

Goats are being used to control brush and thereby reduce the risk of fire. They thrive on rough, rocky land and the browse that poses the highest fire hazard. Goats can be an effective, economical, and environmentally sound solution to the problem of establishing fire breaks on such land.

Hogs can be used as self-motivated bulldozers to clear land of brush and open it up for cultivation. They can also glean fields after harvest or turn over compost and hasten its readiness for use as fertilizer. As omnivores, hogs are able to forage for much of their diet at the same time they are performing useful work in land management.

Draft power and transportation are other important services provided by cattle, horses, donkeys, and mules. Globally, oxen are the most widely used draft animal, though horses are far more common in North America. The common perception of Amish or Mennonites as the only farmers using horse teams is erroneous. More and more people are coming to appreciate the versatility, usefulness, and economy of animal power, particularly given the rising costs of fossil fuels. Draft animals are increasingly being used in selective logging operations on private, federal, and state lands because of the minimal environmental damage they impart to the soil and the remaining trees.

Interest is growing in the use of livestock as part of a system of biological pest control. Swine and poultry have traditionally been kept in orchards to control pests through the shifting of orchard debris and the eating of windfall fruit, grubs, weeds, and other pests. Before the introduction of heavy pesticide use in fruit production, sheep were often pastured in orchards; with organic production, they can again be used for grass and weed control. As a specific example, St. Croix sheep are now being used to control pests in organic macadamia nut plantations in Hawaii.

Figure 1.1. Galloway bull.

Using animal services is doubly beneficial. The services are in themselves positive, and they also replace expensive or potentially detrimental inputs (such as chemical pesticides), high energy use (such as mowing) or labor intensive practices (turning compost or clearing land) — while at the same time the animals are producing marketable food and fiber products.

When the value of animal services is understood, the complicated and rewarding interconnection between human beings and livestock becomes more obvious. Agricultural systems that use these complex interrelationships of people, livestock, and specific environments to the fullest extent are also the ones that benefit most from the availability of traditional breeds of livestock.

Chapter 2

The Importance of Genetic Diversity

By definition, genetic diversity within a species is the presence of a large number of genetic variants for each of its characteristics. This variability is significant because it allows the species to adapt to changes in environments or other pressures by selection for the most successful variants. As an example, variation in hair length in a population could allow for the selection of individuals with longer, thicker hair over those with short, thin hair should the climate become colder.

The opposite of genetic diversity is genetic uniformity. A population that is genetically uniform may be exquisitely suited to a particular environment. Unfortunately, specialization frequently results in an inability to meet the challenges imposed by any change in the environment or in selection goals. A truly uniform population has no reserve of options for change.

The global importance of genetic diversity is widely recognized as it relates to the wild realm — rain forests, wetlands, tidal marshes, and prairies. Diversity of habitats, species, and genes allows evolution to continue apace, and makes possible the constant adaptations to slight or marked changes in the environment that are necessary for interactive life forms to continue living and functioning together.

Similarly, agriculture depends on genetic diversity for its long term health and stability. The fundamental difference between agricultural and other biological systems is the extensive human selection at work. Habitats within agriculture are essentially the result of human activity, and diversity of such habitats must be protected to ensure the long term survival of genetic diversity in both domestic animals and plants.

The accomplishments of modern North American agriculture have been made possible through the selection and use of genetic diversity in animals and plants from around the world, coupled with various modern technologies. Future selection of different characteristics and development of new breeds are completely dependent on the presence of genetic variation within existing populations. While livestock breeders in North America have historically been able to import the genetic diversity they needed, much of that diversity has now been extinguished. We can no longer assume that someone else will have the genetic resources we need for the future. Stewardship of existing North American genetic resources must become a priority.

The Expression of Diversity in Livestock

An examination of the contrasts between domestic and wild animal species provides a useful starting point for a discussion of genetic diversity in livestock.

In wild species, the advantage goes to animals which are best suited to a particular environment. The most successful animals reproduce most frequently and contribute most to the genetic pool, thereby ensuring the continuation of the successful attributes. Different environments provide opportunities for diversity to be expressed in many different ways. These different expressions can result in the divergence of populations into distinct subspecies. The tiger, with its Siberian, Bengal, Sumatran, Chinese, and Korean subspecies, is a good example.

Genetic variation in domesticated animals is manifest in fundamentally different ways than in wild animals, due largely to the impact of human selection. Even the term "species" is somewhat awkward when applied to domesticated animals, since most livestock species have had inputs from more than one ancestral species, most of which are now extinct. (As a result, the domesticated animals are the only living representatives of some of these lineages, and this makes them a critical component of the overall biodiversity of life on earth.)

The primary taxonomic unit of variation in domestic animals is the breed, which roughly coincides with the subspecies in wild animals. A breed is a group of animals which may be readily distinguished from other members of the species and which are consistently within a relatively narrow range of parameters: when bred to one another, members of the breed reproduce this distinguishing type. That is, like begets like, a simple but widely accepted definition of breed.

Breeds were created by isolation and divergence. Geographic isolation of small populations, coupled with selection by humans and the environment, caused certain combinations of traits to become common throughout regional populations. Continued regional isolation

8

concentrated these genetic peculiarities, which then became the hall-marks of distinct populations, or breeds. Human selection subsequently increased uniformity within breeds and distinctions between breeds. The dynamic process of breed evolution continues in response to both human and natural selection.

It is important to realize that a breed is defined by more than its external physical qualities. Breeds are also defined by specific, complex behaviors and other heritable traits. All of these characteristics (which collectively are called the phenotype of the animal or the breed) are not easily attributed to specific, identifiable genes. Rather, they are the result of unique gene configurations and combinations developed through generations of reproductive isolation.

When variations occur regularly within a breed, usually denoting differences in superficial characteristics such as color or hair, they are described by the term "variety." The term "strain" refers to a specific family or bloodline that is more closely related genetically than is the breed as a whole.

The formal development of breeds and an appreciation of the breed concept is a recent phenomenon and is primarily a product of western culture. Breed types have existed for millennia, due largely to geographic isolation, but deliberate selective breeding for fixed types only began in the 1500s and 1600s. Breeds which resulted from early, intentional selection include Spanish horses, Merino sheep, and Devon cattle.

In the 1700s, breeders developed a better understanding of reproduction and transmission of characteristics from generation to generation. This understanding made possible the formal organization of breeds, including the formulation of criteria for inclusion or exclusion of animals into the breed and the keeping of individual pedigrees. These records were called stud books for horses, herd books for cattle and swine, and flock books for sheep. The genetic isolation of breeds was thus codified. Reproductive isolation caused by geography gave way to isolation based on artificial human selection and maintained by specific breeding practices.

Since livestock breeds were developed to be different from one another and have been maintained in isolation from one another, they are identifiable packages of distinct genetic content and configuration. The number of breeds and the numbers of animals within the breeds are good indicators of the status of genetic diversity within each livestock species.

Chapter 3

Genetic Erosion in North American Livestock

It is through an appreciation of breed population dynamics that the status of genetic diversity can best be understood. Livestock breeds are both the units of most significant genetic variation in domestic animals and the units about which information is most readily available.

When a breed declines in numbers, specific genes as well as specific gene combinations within the breed become less common. Some genetic information may be lost, and if the decline persists, it is certain that some genes and gene combinations will cease to exist within the breed. If the breed becomes extinct, then both the specific genes as well as specific and intricate gene combinations in that breed are lost to the species as a whole.

Genetic erosion by breed reduction or extinction can be counteracted by timely action, but effective conservation efforts can only be implemented if breed status is understood. A complete evaluation of livestock breeds includes an inventory of the number of breeds per species and the number of animals per breed. Equally important is the genetic breadth of the breed, the numbers of parents for each successive generation, and changes in the selection goals or breeding practices that are occurring. Furthermore, one must know the range of the needs in agriculture and how these needs may be met by various breeds.

The number of breeds within a species and their relative numerical strength is a useful indicator of the diversity available to that species. The domination of a livestock species by a single breed or a few breeds is a recent phenomenon. For example, the Holstein breed exceeds all other cattle breeds in the quantity of milk produced per cow, and it is now the dominant dairy breed around the world. The popularity and prevalence of this breed has come at the expense of most other dairy breeds, several of which are threatened with extinction. Yet the Holstein is a specialized animal, dependent on high quality feed and intensive management. Its advantages decline under lower input systems, where other breeds may be more efficient. The genetic diversity provided by a variety of cattle breeds, to fit a range of resources and management programs, is necessary for a secure global dairy industry.

Swine provide another example of reduced diversity as a result of the loss of entire breeds (see Appendix I). Breed loss has occurred through extinction and also through the processes of crossbreeding and the development of new breeds. While the most significant and obvious genetic loss is total extinction, genetic dilution through the combination of breeds may also remove unique gene combinations and decrease the integrity of the original genetic package available to the species.

The infusion of outside blood dilutes the genetic distinctiveness of a breed. An example is the introduction of Australian Illawara cattle into the American Milking Shorthorn breed in the 1960s to increase milk production. Subsequently, the Red and White Holstein was also introduced to boost production still further. The pre-Illawara strain of Milking Shorthorn is now extremely rare, threatening the loss of unique genetic combinations within the breed.

Figure 3.1. Essex and Suffolk — two extinct breeds of swine.

Chapter 4

The Agricultural Context of Genetic Erosion

Rapid genetic erosion is occurring in all of the livestock species of North America to the extent that nearly 80 livestock breeds are in decline or in danger of extinction (see Section II for details).

C. M. A. Baker and C. Manwell have said, "It is often assumed that the spread or decline of a breed is solely or mainly because of its relative merit. In fact, a complicated web of interacting socio-economic reasons is involved, and merit (or lack thereof) may make a relatively small contribution."[1]

This web of factors is readily observed in North America today: uniform industrial selection; substitution of nonrenewable resources for animals' natural abilities; devaluation of the purebred; consolidation of livestock resources; and attitudes favoring standardization. These factors apply generally to all livestock species and directly or indirectly have led to loss of genetic diversity.

Uniform Industrial Selection

Traditionally, many breeds were utilized in livestock agriculture and they all served more than one purpose. Current selection has generally been concentrated on a single breed or type for each animal product. As a result, a single breed or at best a few breeds have become dominant. These highly selected populations are known as industrial breeds.

The high production levels of industrial stocks are not to be disparaged. Industrial livestock provide most of the animal products in the North American diet. At the same time, however, these animals — incredibly successful though they be — are functioning in a very recently developed, expensive, and specialized environment, one that is unique in agricultural history.

Industrial selection of production animals is increasingly narrow. Selection is made for a very few factors — rapid growth rate with early maturation, early reproduction with large litters, and feed conversion efficiency based on the use of a high grain diet. Industrial stocks are selected to fit the system precisely and to show predictable characteristics. When an individual's output drops below predicted levels, uniformity allows replacement with an identical production unit.

New animal breeding technologies mean few geographical limits to the reproduction of animals. Reproductive technologies, including artificial insemination, embryo transfer, embryo splitting, and cloning have the potential to reproduce the best individuals many times over their natural capacity. As fewer and fewer animals have been used for breeding, a breed's genetic base is narrowed with every generation. The losses are acute on the male side since industrial stocks rely on only a few male bloodlines; limited sire lines mean few grandsires and great-grandsires. Selection for uniformity concentrates not only positive genetic characteristics, but also the negative traits.

The drive toward uniformity has become a problem at the species level. Not only are individuals in a breed increasingly uniform, but all commercial breeds within a species are being selected toward the highest producing types. This is true of beef cattle, sheep, and swine — all selected toward a standard carcass profile, rapid gain, and efficient utilization of high concentrate feed. In dairy cattle all breeds are selected toward the Holstein type, while riding horses are now being selected toward the Thoroughbred type. The resulting loss of variation is a significant limitation to future selection for differing environments, levels of input, uses, products, or other unforeseen needs.

Substitution of Nonrenewable Resources for Natural Abilities

Industrial selection largely ignores the innate abilities of livestock, now made redundant through substitution of capital, energy, and other inputs. The breeds which are climate adapted, show strong maternal instincts, and thrive under extensive husbandry are not relevant to current intensive industrial production systems and have generally been cast aside.

Modern agriculture has used a variety of inputs to support and expand production levels. Animal feed now consists of high energy grain and protein supplements which are grown, processed, and transported specifically for animals. These feeds are frequently coupled with additives and growth enhancers. Single purpose, high-tech housing for industrial animal production has removed the need for climate adaptations present in animals that thrive outdoors.

Intensive husbandry creates an increased need for veterinary support and monitoring of health status. Due to the concentration of large numbers of animals, any infectious diseases or imbalance in nutrition or environment will have a rapid and dramatic impact. Parasitacides are administered routinely, selecting against genetic resistance and the husbandry practices which can control parasites. Increased management is also required for successful reproduction, and includes fertility enhancement, birthing assistance, and the hand rearing of young.

Manure, a valued resource on the diversified farm, is a waste product in modern industrial systems. Problems with disposal are now a major cause of surface and ground water pollution.

Devaluation of the Purebred

"Hybrid vigor" is the performance boost attained through crossing distantly related parents. Also called heterosis, hybrid vigor is the foundation of modern commercial livestock production. It is now assumed that the crossbred will outperform the purebred. In the rush to

Figure 4.1. Cleveland Bay stallion.

use crossbreeding, however, the necessity of maintaining genetically distinct parent breeds has been widely ignored. If all breeds become uniform, through selection or through crossbreeding, the potential benefits of hybrid vigor will be greatly diminished.

Many purebred animals, particularly females, have been siphoned from purebreeding to crossbreeding programs. These programs may use endangered breeds to introduce characteristics such as maternal abilities or, more often, may use commercial breeds to "improve" the endangered breeds. Crossbreeding may be a logical choice for breeders who want to meet a current market demand, but successful crossbreeding has also been the demise of many unique and useful breeds. For example, owners of purebred Cleveland Bay mares often breed them to Thoroughbred rather than to Cleveland Bay stallions, since there is currently a far greater demand for crossbreds than for purebreds. Texas Longhorns were nearly bred out of existence due to their excellent production of crossbred calves. Only a few breeders kept purebreds, understanding that the contribution of the pure old Spanish Texas Longhorn cow was essential to the excellence of the crossbred.

Decreasing emphasis on purebred stocks has also resulted in a diminished appreciation of the art of livestock breeding. Endangered are the host of skills that characterize the talented livestock breeder, including the ability to develop a long term breeding program and to evaluate individuals of each generation as part of a herd and breed. These skills have increasingly been replaced by computer predicted performance of a single task.

Consolidation of Livestock Resources

Since World War II all agricultural resources, including livestock, have become consolidated into fewer units of larger size. As a result, genetic resources have also been concentrated and many non-industrial stocks have been lost.

While North Americans have enjoyed an abundance of cheap and varied foods as a benefit of modern production and distribution systems, there have also been significant unanticipated consequences. The increasing size and specialization of agricultural operations have meant the separation of livestock production from other agricultural processes, such as food crop and forage production. Livestock is now considered an end product only, rather than an integral part of a diversified agricultural system.

Much of our food is produced by a few international conglomerates. The swine and poultry industries are particularly concentrated and are characterized by a vertical relationship in which the parent company owns genetic stocks and makes all breeding decisions, while the farmer is only a contract grower of stocks provided.

Dairy production is still in the hands of individual farmers, although the milk produced is bought by a few large processors. Beef and lamb production is likewise characterized by a multitude of smaller producers as well as the giant corporate producers, but the diversity possible with such decentralized production has been counterbalanced by large centralized processing structures. The discounted price paid to producers of non-conforming stock serves to impose uniformity throughout the entire system.

The consolidation of breeding, production, and processing has encouraged a move toward production animals which are uniform, interchangeable units. The impact on livestock breeds has been tremendous. Those breeds which perform best under industrial conditions have been further modified to excel when given additional resource inputs such as feed supplements, growth enhancers, sophisticated housing, and intensive husbandry. The vast majority of our food producing animals are those which are selected only for industrial conditions.

Throughout history, agriculture has been marked by the genius of millions of creative and skilled individuals. Consolidation has meant a reduction in the number of decision makers in agriculture. For example, the September 1992 *North Carolina Pork Report* stated that in 1967 there were more than 70 breeders of purebred swine in North Carolina; in 1990, there were fewer than 20, despite the burgeoning swine industry in the state.

Attitudes Favoring Standardization

Inseparable from these trends in modern agriculture are the attitudes which support it, attitudes which favor increased uniformity of livestock breeds and management systems. In its acceptance of uniform, high input livestock production systems, livestock agriculture may inadvertently destroy the very base of its own success — genetic diversity.

The single system favored by industrial producers and processors is the use of intensive management for the maximization of output. This has been assumed to be the only modern way to produce livestock, and the single system appropriate for all climates and geographies, and for the entire future of society.

Research has accepted this assumption rather than challenged it. While the questions of researchers are valid, they are narrowly focused and the answers which are generated are likewise narrow. The results tend to be more widely implemented and fostered than the original questions and assumptions would warrant. As a result, agricultural systems become more similar, and the choices of acceptable genetic resources also become increasingly narrow. The phenomenon of institutional research and extension has thus come to favor the elimination of many packages of genetic variation in the interests of perceived progress.

During the last fifty years, for example, there has been practically no research on the production of livestock on low input, forage based systems. One element in today's dairy crisis is the lack of data on milk production from grass fed cattle, even though dairy breeds were traditionally selected to produce milk on grass alone. This lower cost production system is a feasible option for many farmers today, but the research to support its implementation remains to be done.

If the assumptions that undergird modern industrial agriculture — such as the continued availability of cheap energy — were to change, then it is reasonable to expect that the animals necessary in a future agriculture would be different than those functioning well today. It is for this reason that the rare breeds need to be kept intact as *functioning and viable genetic units* which can be used in the future.

This is a time of instability and change in agriculture. The lack of economic opportunity in farming is leading many people to diversify and experiment with alternative species, breeds, and systems as they try to make a living on the farm. There is growing interest in raising livestock in low-input systems, and as a result, research interest in forage efficiency is increasing. The use of livestock on small-scale diversified farms is also growing. These trends favor the use and resulting conservation of genetic diversity in livestock.

---

[1] C. M. A. Baker and C. Manwell, "Population Genetics, Molecular Markers and Gene Conservation of Bovine Breeds" in C. G. Hickman, ed., *Cattle Genetic Resources*, Elsevier Science Publishers (Amsterdam, 1991).

Chapter 5

The Conservation of Livestock Genetic Diversity

Livestock genetic diversity — as represented by a wide variety of genetically distinct breeds — must be conserved to meet six societal needs: food security, economic opportunity, environmental stewardship, scientific knowledge, cultural and historical preservation, and ethical responsibility.

Food Security

The very fabric of North American society depends on a stable food supply, which assumes a continuation of domestic agriculture. At risk is the genetic breadth required to produce an array of foods, in a variety of climates, utilizing a variety of systems. Genetic diversity is also the basis for response to future environmental challenges, such as global warming, evolving pests and diseases, and availability of energy. Along with market demands and human needs, these challenges are profoundly unpredictable.

The necessity of genetic diversity in the food crops is well illustrated. The Irish Potato Famine of the 1840s was caused by *Phytophtora infestans*, a blight to which the genetically uniform Irish potato crop was not resistant. The blight destroyed potatoes for five years, with staggering social consequence — the dislocation or death of millions of people. Luckily, there were potatoes in Mexico and the Andean countries which were resistant to the blight. It was only this resistance that allowed potatoes to become a major food crop in the world today.

When stripe rust threatened the wheat crop in the northwestern United States during the 1960s, resistance was discovered in a Turkish wheat which, though brought to the United States in 1948, had been ignored since it had poor baking qualities, lacked winter hardiness and was generally "miserable looking." Yet this wheat was resistant not only to stripe rust, but also bunt, flag smut and snow mould. It is now used in all wheat breeding programs in the northwestern United States, saving farmers millions of dollars each year.[1]

Examples of such disasters for livestock are also compelling. Parasite control in sheep has been a universal management problem. Modern parasiticides have eliminated the need to select for parasite resistance, but suddenly the literature is documenting sheep parasites with complete resistance to current drugs. Large areas of sheep range in Australia have been depopulated of sheep because of the ravages of parasites. Now this parasiticide resistance is showing up in North America. Gulf Coast Native sheep and Caribbean hair sheep show remarkable genetic parasite resistance, an adaptation to the heat, humidity, and parasite load of their native habitats. Utilizing genetic resistance may be the preferred way to combat parasites rather than the development of yet another new drug to which parasites will eventually and assuredly become resistant.

Most commercial swine on this continent are susceptible to *Escherichia coli* scours, while certain genetic strains of Chinese hogs are not. The Chinese hogs are very different in appearance and performance characteristics than the North American swine. But if the choice comes down to a dead North American hog or a live Chinese hog, the Chinese hog will certainly win — slab sides, fat back, wrinkles and all.

An old adage warns against "putting all eggs in one basket." A genetically uniform livestock and/or crop base does just this. Diversity is essential for long term food security.

Economic Opportunity

There is tremendous long-term economic potential from breed conservation. Many rare breeds yield high value products, such as naturally colored wool for handspinning, free range and grass fed meat, and unusual cheeses which can be marketed into specialty niches.

Rare breeds may also be a foundation for the development of domestic industries to serve markets which now rely on imports. For example, North Americans now import almost all of the sheep milk cheeses, such as feta and roquefort, and over 10 percent of the lamb consumed here; there is opportunity for domestic economic expansion.

Genetic conservation makes possible the development of new breeds. Some recent North American examples include Santa Gertrudis cattle (a blend of Zebu and Shorthorn), Senepol cattle (a blend of N'Dama and Red Poll), and Katahdin sheep (a blend of Caribbean hair sheep, Wiltshire, and wooled breeds), all of which were developed to meet the market demand for a quality carcass produced under unusual climatic constraints. Unique genetic combinations in endangered breeds — particularly those breeds which are distantly related to commercial stocks — must be conserved for this opportunity to be protected.

Breeds which are rare today may carry traits which will be of commercial importance tomorrow. The Finn sheep, for example, was discarded by commercial producers earlier this century and kept only by Finnish peasants. Today the Finn's fecundity — its ability to produce litters of lambs instead of singles or twins — is being widely utilized in the sheep industry.

Environmental Stewardship

Agriculture is the chief human interaction with the environment. We must maintain the genetic resources to allow for agriculture's adaptation to environmental changes; to improve the environmental sustainability of agricultural production; and to substitute livestock services and products for environmentally and economically costly use of chemicals, energy, and other inputs. Increasingly these alternatives make economic as well as environmental sense.

In addition, the properly managed grazing of livestock can be used to recover diversity in damaged habitats, such as wetlands, prairies and grasslands. The use of forage crops and permanent pasture aid in the recovery of abused and eroded crop lands. Grazing is essential to the longterm health of grasslands, and grasslands cover more global land surface than any other ecosystem. Grasslands are an important collector of solar energy and are essential in global recycling systems for energy, water, minerals, and oxygen. Given the extinction of many wild herbivores, their domestic descendants — livestock — are of great ecological importance.

Scientific Knowledge

A full understanding of the animal kingdom, to which humans belong, requires the protection of maximum genetic diversity. Many rare breeds are biologically unusual and provide opportunities to study adaptation, disease and parasite resistance, reproductive differences, feed utilization under a variety of forage systems, and human disease. The Ossabaw Island hog, for example, is a research model for non-insulin dependent diabetes. Myotonic goats are a similar model for human *myotonia congenita*. Gulf Coast Native sheep and Florida Cracker cattle exhibit high resistance to parasites. North Ronaldsay sheep on the Scottish Orkney Islands subsist on a diet primarily made up of seaweed, a very unusual adaptation for metabolizing high levels of dietary sodium and copper.

Figure 5.1. Merino ram.

Cultural and Historical Preservation

The root of agriculture is culture. Historic breeds of livestock are the result of human creativity and culture, worthy of being protected along with complex artifacts such as language, works of art, and technological innovations of the past.

Solutions to contemporary problems are often found in records of the past. Many traditional livestock husbandry techniques retain their usefulness today, but the common wisdom of the past is no longer valued or taught in colleges. Our responsibility to future generations requires us to pass on as complete an agricultural record as possible, giving farmers the opportunity to learn from past generations and use the heritage breeds which have been the basis for North American agriculture.

Ethical Responsibility

Stewardship of the Earth includes not only the myriad species of wild animals, plants and habitats, but also the domestic animals and plants which are part of the biological web of life. Those who appreciate the role of livestock in conserving the environment, providing services, food and other products, and companionship believe that domestic animals have a right to continued existence as do wild species. Domestic animals are the first animals we learn as children and the subject of most nursery rhymes and children's stories. Human beings have a particular obligation to protect the domestic species which have been our partners for so many centuries of coevolution and interdependence.

---

[1]Cary Fowler and Pat Mooney, *Shattering: Food, Politics, and the Loss of Genetic Diversity*, University of Arizona Press (Tucson, AZ, 1990).

Section II

A North American Livestock Census

Chapter 6

The Census

In 1985, the American Livestock Breeds Conservancy (ALBC) conducted the first national livestock breeds census since the USDA abandoned such record keeping for specific breeds early in this century. The present census continues the important work of determining livestock breed status in North America with information from 1990. It includes both methodology and data from the original 1985 report, written by Elizabeth Henson, then director of ALBC.

The North American Livestock Census is the only research report of its kind to be published in the United States and offers research methods which are a global model for the work of livestock conservation.

North America is the topic of the census because it is in many ways a single agricultural unit, with breed populations shared between Canada and the United States. Livestock can generally be moved across the border unimpeded, so the exchange of breeding stock has been widely practiced. Most animals are registered only in Canada or in the United States, so it is possible to gather figures for each country and then add these for a continental total.

The primary survey population for this census was the many livestock breed associations in North America. Breed associations are groups of breeders and other interested people with an affinity for a particular breed of livestock. Associations foster communication and serve as a forum for discussion of breed goals and breed promotion. An essential role of most breed associations is the registration of purebred animals by name, pedigree, and date of birth, with the assignment of a registration number in the breed flock book, herd book, or stud book. Registration identifies animals as members of the breed and allows for tracking numerical and genetic trends within the population.

Industry trade groups, which also keep breed information and monitor trends, were another source of census information. These include the American Horse Council, the American Sheep Industry Association, the Canadian Livestock Record Corporation (the national registry for most Canadian livestock breeds), the National Cattlemen's Association, and the National Pedigree Livestock Council. Also helpful were farming and livestock publications, such as *Hoard's Dairyman, The Pork Report, The Shepherd, New Farm, Small Farm Today,* and *The Stockman Grass Farmer.*

In addition, individual breeders across North America were surveyed to provide a range of perspectives about breed status and trends. Contact with individuals was necessary for those breeds lacking an active breed association, but breeders' opinions were also important to an understanding of trends within even the most active breed associations and for the most numerically strong breeds.

Methods

Research for the North American Livestock Census was conducted between September 1990 and September 1992. Research began with mail surveys to all breed associations in North America. Follow-up telephone conversations were made beginning in the summer of 1991. Contacts with individual breeders were made in the spring and summer of 1992. Research from published data was done throughout the entire period.

The following types of information were gathered: registration figures for 1990 in both the United States and Canada; estimates of North American and global populations; numbers of breeders and association members in North America; cumulative registrations; and registration policies (such as open or closed herd books, grading up programs, and use of artificial insemination and embryo transfer). Not all of this information was available for all breeds or even all species, nor is it listed for all species in this report.

Annual purebred registration figures are the primary indicator of the reproductive status of a breed. Generally, the number of registrations in a given year reflects the number of purebreds born which are likely to be retained for breeding. Registrations measure the general trend of purebred reproduction versus crossbreeding or non-reproduction, which would be obscured if the total adult breeding population (or the number of breeding age females) was instead the reference figure. In addition, registrations are a useful estimate of general activity among breed association membership, since people who take the time and resources to register animals are also those most likely to have a long term commitment to the breed.

Registration figures from the first year or two of a registry's operation should be interpreted with caution. In the first years of operation of a new herd book it is usual for many adults to be registered as the foundation stock of the breed. The registration of these foundation animals inflates the annual numbers beyond the number of purebred offspring also registered. The new herd book for the Florida Cracker cattle, for example, lists approximate registration figures that are closer to a breed total than the number of purebred calves born in 1990. A comparison of the date of registry founding and cumulative registrations, when available, will clarify the situation.

Published information and breed association data were used to make estimates of the total population of each breed in the United States, Canada, and worldwide when possible. This information is most readily available for horses and cattle. Figures on cumulative registrations were also obtained as a measure of historic breed popularity in an effort to track trends.

The number of active breeders was obtained as another indicator of the overall level of breeding activity. Given the same number of animals, a larger number of breeders puts a breed in a stronger position than does fewer. Having the breed dispersed in several herds reduces the impact of loss of a single herd due to local disease, dispersal, or disaster. It also maximizes diversity due to the general customs of breeding; one breeder with a large herd will use fewer males (and therefore less genetic diversity) than will several breeders with smaller herds, even though the total breed population may be the same.

Results

Census results have been organized by species and are found in the following chapters. Each species chapter includes a chart of breed populations, commentary on use in agriculture, an analysis of recent trends, and a complete list of breed associations in North America. Conservation priorities have been determined according to the genetic uniqueness of a breed, the status of the breed in North America and globally, and the trends which have affected the breed over the past twenty years.

Chapter 7

Asses

Asses (*Equus asinus*) are characterized by a loud braying voice, long ears, upright mane, and tufted tail. Both tough and strong, the ass is perhaps the hardiest of all livestock species.

Asses have been used for centuries for riding, packing, and draft power, and they are still important in many parts of the world. Another historical use, and one of particular importance in the United States, has been the production of mules. Mules result from the mating of a jack (male ass) to a mare (female horse). Mules are exceptional work animals, larger and faster than asses, and stronger and sturdier than horses.

Figure 7.1. Mammoth Jackstock.

31

While the ass species is not globally threatened, some domestic breeds and wild asses are near extinction. Of particular concern in North America is the status of the improved breeds, generally large in size, which were developed for the production of draft mules.

Asses are generally called donkeys in North America. The breeds are differentiated primarily by size, though they also have genetically different origins. The American Mammoth Jackstock, the largest breed, stands 56/58–64 inches (14/14.2–16 hands) high at the withers. Large Standard donkeys are 48–56 inches (12–14/14.2 hands) and Standard donkeys 36–48 inches (9–12 hands) high. Miniature donkeys are 36 inches or less at the withers. The Spotted Ass is a color breed, including those animals of any donkey breed with spotted coats.

The Large Breeds
American Mammoth Jackstock and Poitou

The American Mammoth Jackstock breed was first developed during the late 1700s and early 1800s by George Washington, Henry Clay, and other Southern agriculturalists. They crossed several types of asses, primarily of Spanish origin, and selected for large jacks which would in turn produce powerful work mules. The result was the American Mammoth Jackstock, one of the finest mule-producing ass breeds in the world. Kentucky, Missouri, and Tennessee became the breeding centers for Mammoth Jackstock, and mules were supplied to farmers in the Southeast and the West and to the United States Army. Peak years of mule use were 1880–1925.

Agriculture and war have always provided the primary markets for mules and, therefore, for American Mammoth Jackstock. By the middle of the twentieth century, animal power in both agriculture and the military was replaced with machine power, and the demand for Mammoth Jackstock plummeted. During the 1950s and 1960s, only a handful of dedicated breeders kept the breed alive.

The last twenty years have seen a revival of interest in American Mammoth Jackstock, particularly among younger people. This revival may be attributed to the renewed interest in farming with draft animals, the growing market for riding mules, and to a lesser extent to the show ring. About one hundred Mammoth Jackstock foals were registered during 1990, but the global population still numbers only a few hundred animals. The American Mammoth Jackstock breed is found almost exclusively in America; the Canadian population of 50–60 animals is the largest outside of the United States.

The Poitou, an ancient French ass breed, has also been known for its ability to produce excellent mules. The Poitou was described as early as the twelfth century in southwestern France. It is quite distinctive in appearance, with a very heavy build and a long, tangled coat.

Poitou mules were ridden by magistrates and clergy, perhaps by the popes themselves. Control of breeding stock was tightly held in the Poitou region of France, keeping breed characteristics unchanged for centuries.

In the early 1900s there were hundreds of Poitous, but the shift from animal to machine power after the First World War caused a drastic decline in demand for mules. Primitive management techniques and lack of interest nearly led to the extinction of the breed. By the late 1970s there were only 50 Poitou asses left in the world.

During the 1980s, efforts to conserve the Poitou became organized and are now coordinated by the French organization *La Sabaud* (The Association to Save the Poitou Donkey), with some assistance from the International Donkey Protection Trust in the United Kingdom. Progress is being made in the identification and registration of all animals, and in the use of artificial insemination to increase the population. The breed is still critically rare, with fewer than 100 animals worldwide, but it now stands an increasing chance of survival. Conservation of the Poitou centers in France. There are fewer than twelve Poitous in North America, closely held in a privately managed breeding program.

The American Mammoth Jackstock and the Poitou Ass are the most genetically significant and endangered North American ass breeds. They are a global conservation priority.

Large Standard and Standard Donkeys

Large Standard and Standard Donkeys are the common donkeys used around the world. In North America, donkeys of intermediate size are used for driving, packing, and other forms of recreation, as well as for the production of medium-sized mules. Large Standards, bred with riding horses, produce riding mules of generally lighter type than those bred from Mammoth Jacks.

A new use for Large Standard and Standard donkeys is as guardians for sheep, goats, and other small animals. Donkeys have an instinctive distrust of dogs and coyotes, and many will defend themselves and their herd from predators. More research is needed about training methods for guard donkeys, but this market may hold great potential.

Burro is the term used to describe the feral donkey of the western United States. Mexican donkeys were used throughout the Southwest in the latter half of the nineteenth century, but they were displaced when the gold rushes came to an end. Abandoned animals formed free roaming burro populations in many desert areas.

Feral burros (and feral horses) on public lands in the United States were given federal protection in 1971, but changing land management goals of the various federal agencies over the past twenty years have resulted in a steady reduction in the number of herds and in herd sizes.

Thousands of burros have been removed from the open range and adopted by private owners, who were then able to register them (usually as Standard donkeys) with the American Donkey and Mule Society. In a few generations of redomestication, burros removed from wild populations may lose genetic uniqueness attained from natural selection in rigorous desert environments. Only by maintaining some free roaming burro populations can the genetic information of this exceptionally hardy animal be conserved.

Miniature Donkeys

Miniature donkeys were imported from Italy beginning in 1929. The first importer was Robert Green, a stock broker with a farm in New Jersey. He bought seven Sardinian asses, sight unseen, while on a trip to Europe. A few other families also imported donkeys, keeping them for their own amusement rather than as commercial ventures.

Even limited publicity on the donkeys in the 1930s attracted great interest, but there were never enough animals in the United States to fill the demand. In fact, not until the 1980s did Miniature donkeys experience a dramatic growth in population. Now they are widely promoted as companion animals and can also be used for driving. Miniatures are generally too small to serve as guard donkeys.

Though the number of Miniatures is increasing in North America, some genetic concerns lie in the perceived market demand for smaller and smaller donkeys. Selection for size alone can lead to the breeding of animals of inferior health, soundness, and reproductive fitness. Other concerns lie in the lack of experience among many breeders and in the levels of inbreeding in donkey herds in some parts of North America.

The North American population of Miniature donkeys appears to be of greater global importance than earlier recognized, given recent trends to crossbreed the Mediterranean populations of Miniatures for increased size. Though the Miniature donkey is not immediately threatened with extinction, its global status should be carefully monitored and the North American populations conserved.

Spotted Asses

Spotted Asses are donkeys of any size which have spots. These animals may be registered in both the regular breed and the color registries. Spotted animals are growing in popularity and this interest may increase the overall percentage of Standard and Large Standard donkeys which are registered. The American Council of Spotted Asses also works to promote the use of donkeys as companion animals and in recreation and agriculture.

Table 7.1
Ass Registrations

It is difficult to determine breed populations of asses in North America, as only a small percentage of animals are registered. Registration figures for Miniature donkeys and for American Mammoth Jackstock may be most indicative of true numbers, since buyers of these higher priced individuals desire registered animals. The intermediate size breeds are least likely to be registered, but they are also the most abundant, both globally and in North America. Figures from Canada were unavailable.

Breed	Number of Registrations 1990	Cumulative	Estimated Global Population	Data Source[1]
All donkeys	Unavailable	12,187	40,000,000[a]	p, s
American Mammoth Jackstock	110[b]	38,390	500	s, t
Miniature Donkey	614[b]		10,000	s, t
Poitou Ass	1		100	p, t
Spotted Ass	450		20,000	s
Large Standard and Standard Donkeys	350[b]			s, t

[1] p = published information; s = survey; t = telephone interview
[a] FAO estimate, 1989
[b] Estimate

Conservation Priority Ass Breeds

Critical: Fewer than 200 annual registrations in North America and an estimated global population of less than 2,000.

American Mammoth Jackstock *
Poitou Ass

Watch: Fewer than 2,500 annual registrations in North America and an estimated global population of less than 10,000.

Miniature Donkey

* Unique to North America

35

Ass Breed Associations

(The date in parenthesis is the year the association was founded.)

The American **Donkey & Mule** Society (1967), 2901 N Elm, Denton, TX 76201; 817-382-6845.

The Canadian **Donkey & Mule** Association, c/o Anne Roszel, Route 1, Priceville, ON N0C 1K0, Canada; 519-369-5989.

The **Donkey** Sanctuary and International Donkey Protection Trust (1969), Sidmouth, Devon, EX10 0NU, England.

The **American Mammoth Jackstock** Registry (1888), 6513 W Laurel Rd, London, KY 40741-9717; Marlene Patton, 1-800-531-9932, 606-878-0486.

The International Registry of **American Mammoth Jackstock** and the American Mammmoth Jackstock Journal (1992), PO Box 38, Floyd's Knob, IN 47119; 502-894-9830.

The American Mustang and **Burro** Association, PO Box 788, Lincoln, CA 95648.

National **Miniature Donkey** Association (1990), RR 1 Box 472, Dewey Rd, Rome, NY 13440; 315-336-0154.

The American Council of **Spotted Asses** (1962), PO Box 121, New Melle, MO 63365; 314-828-5100.

Figure 7.2   Poitou ass.

Chapter 8

Cattle

Cattle (*Bos taurus* and *Bos indicus*) have found a place in most societies around the globe as a measure of food security, wealth, and spirituality. In North America, cattle and cattle raising have traditionally been highly esteemed, and individual animals are often of great value. These two factors have helped to support and maintain the production of purebred cattle as an important agricultural enterprise.

Cattle and calves are the leading agricultural commodity in the United States and Canada. According to Roger Strickland of the United States Department of Agriculture's Economic Research Service, livestock and products accounted for 53 percent, or $89.6 billion, of the nearly $170 billion in agricultural cash receipts for 1990. In 33 states,

Figure 8.1. Milking Devon cattle.

livestock was the number one commodity. Cattle and calves accounted for 23.3 percent of United States farm receipts, and dairy products accounted for 11.8 percent, making cattle the source for 35.1 percent of farm income.

Beef Cattle

A wide array of cattle breeds are present in North America, especially among those selected for beef. The North American cattle industry was based historically on Spanish cattle in the South and West, and on British breeds — particularly Shorthorn, Hereford, and Angus — in the East. At the beginning of the twentieth century, the Indian Zebu breeds, and, to a lesser extent, African breeds were introduced because of their heat tolerance.

After World War II the beef industry was transformed by the introduction of continental breeds from Europe, such as the Charolais and Simmental. Producers were seeking large framed animals to meet a growing demand for lean, boned beef rather than the traditional cuts of roasts and chops. Importation of a wide variety of breeds continued through the 1960s and 1970s.

The use of European breeds illustrates the importance of genetic diversity to the beef industry. The large frame and other characteristics which made the continental breeds so valuable to American producers resulted from generations of selection by European farmers for large, sturdy draft animals. While the role of oxen in contemporary North America is limited, draft breeds have nonetheless made a significant contribution to the modern beef industry.

Recently imported breeds have been used to develop new, uniquely North American breeds. Zebus, for example, were crossed with British and continental breeds to produce new breed types such as the Brahman and Santa Gertrudis specifically selected for their ability to tolerate the climate of the southern United States. Not all of the imports or the crossbreds have sustained their numbers or their promise, however. In fact, since the 1970s, registrations for some of these breeds have declined. This may be because of general trends in the cattle industry away from purebred stock, or because the newly synthesized breed types can be easily duplicated.

Selection for a large frame has transformed the smaller British breeds. The Angus, for example, has been changed from the small, compact cattle of the 1950s to the huge 2,500 pound animals which now win the blue ribbons in the show ring. There is concern that these large Angus have lost some of their traditional production qualities; they are showing increased calving difficulty due to oversized calves and unsoundness of feet and legs. Yet the breed remains extremely popular within the industry and is well known to the public, in part because of the very successful marketing program of Certified Angus Beef as a premium product.

The beef processors' standard is a very powerful selection force. According to the National Cattlemen's Association report of October 1989, 69 percent of United States beef processing is handled by just four companies. Uniformity of selection for large frame, rapid growth, muscle development (rather than fat deposition), and uniform weight are the goals among most breeds and within breeds. Variations from this norm, such as smaller size, slower maturation, hair, and horns, are discounted by processors seeking a standard meat animal.

The modern beef industry is a testament to the importance of genetic diversity in meeting market changes. The market has benefitted from the importation of breeds from around the world and from aggressive selection of North American stocks. How ironic it would be if the end result of all this genetic diversity was a single standard beef type and the loss of other unique traits, eliminated without recognition of their importance to the future.

Dairy Cattle

Genetic erosion is more obvious among dairy breeds than it is in the beef industry. The production capability of the Holstein overshadows all other dairy breeds, and it is for all practical purposes *the* international dairy breed. No other breed has been so successfully selected to produce such massive volumes of milk. As might be expected, this high productivity is based on maximum nutrition, ample clean water, a non-stressful climate, and excellent husbandry. North American Holsteins have been widely exported to other parts of the world, but their success in foreign production has generally relied on access to imported replacements, the amount of supporting resources, and superior management.

Holstein cows do not have long productive lives and generally are replaced after only two or three lactations. Culled dairy cattle actually supply the largest part of our processed beef. The cost of raising replacement animals for this rapid turnover of productive units is a significant part of the total cost of dairy production.

While the number of Holsteins dwarfs that of other dairy breeds, the disparity is even greater than indicated by the relative numbers of annual purebred registrations. The largest percentage of dairy cattle are not registered purebreds. Of an estimated 9.5 million Holsteins in the United States, only about 15 percent are registered.

The Jersey continues to increase in numbers because of the high percentage of milk solids to water in its milk. The breed has been noted for heat tolerance and fits in well with small scale as well as commercial dairy production. Its popularity indicates that much more is involved in breed dynamics than production alone, since Jerseys continue to be a strong breed numerically in spite of modest total milk yield when compared to the Holstein. The Brown Swiss breed also remains relatively strong, with registration numbers holding steady during the past twenty years. The strength of the Brown Swiss is supported in part by exports to Central America and the Mediterranean, where the breed enjoys an excellent reputation for adaptability and hardiness.

The status of the remaining American dairy breeds is a source of concern. Guernsey registrations in 1990 are less than half the level of 1970. Ayrshire and Milking Shorthorn registrations continue to decline alarmingly. Though these breeds in North America are not in immediate danger of extinction, they are in need of close monitoring and promotion within the agricultural community. As numbers fall within a dairy breed, it becomes less possible to use the statistical evaluation and effective sire selection that has contributed to the dramatic production gains of the dairy industry. Low numbers are a double threat, because as population numbers decrease below levels where effective selection is possible, breed maintenance and improvement become more difficult.

The rarest dairy breeds in North America are the Canadienne, Dutch Belted, and Kerry. The Canadienne, an extremely hardy breed unique to North America, has increased in numbers since the 1980s but is still endangered. Most of the cattle are located in Quebec and the breed society has received some assistance from the provincial government. The Dutch Belted, found only in the United States and The Netherlands, is in dire straits because so few dairy farmers use the breed in production or breed registered stock. The physical attractiveness of the Dutch Belted is sometimes a detriment rather than an advantage, because cattle have been bought by "collectors" who then remove them from the breeding population by crossbreeding or by not registering purebred offspring. The Kerry, which originated in Ireland, is receiving focused conservation attention, especially in Canada, but it is critically rare globally with only a few hundred cattle in existence.

Though rare, the Canadienne, Dutch Belted, and Kerry breeds have much to offer. Their milk is high in solids and excellent for cheese and other dairy manufacture. They retain traits for hardiness, reproductive efficiency, maternal instinct, as well as great foraging capability and feed conversion efficiency. These breeds should certainly be considered for sustainable farming practices such as in grass-based dairying.

Structural problems, particularly low prices, within the United States dairy industry are one cause of the general decline of dairy cattle breeds. At a hearing on boosting minimum milk prices in April 1991, a New York dairy farmer pointed out that ice was selling for 17 cents a pound while his milk sold for 11 cents a pound. He concluded that he would be better off if his cows produced ice.

Because of the investment cost for equipment required to produce and handle Grade A milk on the farm, dairying is increasingly closed to small operators. Ten years ago, in the New York-New Jersey milk marketing area, the top five handlers distributed less than 40 percent of fluid milk sold. Now, nearly 60 percent of fluid milk is sold by the top five dairy companies. The total number of fluid milk handlers in the market area dropped from 63 to 29 in the same ten year period.

There is no question that regulations have resulted in a healthier and more marketable fluid milk product, but the small cheese plants which could utilize the product of small producers have disappeared as milk processing becomes concentrated in fewer food processing corporations. In North Carolina, for example, there is only one market for non-Grade A milk.

Dual Purpose Cattle

Traditionally, all cattle were multi-purpose animals used for milk and meat, and often oxen as well. Over the past two centuries, as livestock breeders became more sophisticated, breeds were selected for more specialized production, some for beef production and others for dairy qualities. These two goals seem to be on the opposite ends of the selection spectrum; beef qualities come at the expense of dairy qualities and vice versa. Until the 1950s and 1960s, there were still several breeds which were maintained as intermediate or dual purpose breeds. Today dual purpose breeds are generally selected for beef production rather than for the combination of traits which made them popular historically.

Devon cattle were imported to North America in the seventeenth century. The Shorthorn, the dominant international breed for more than a century, was imported in the 1800s and 1900s. These two breeds are the most historically prominent dual purpose breeds of cattle. Both breeds were also widely valued as oxen, for their strength, athletic ability, and intelligence. The Shorthorns and Devons of today have been divided into dairy and beef breeds, which explains the recent dates for the establishment of breed associations. However, blood from the milking types is commonly introduced into the beef types as a way to increase the maternal abilities which decline under rigid selection for beef.

The Dexter evolved as an Irish house cow, well suited to small land holdings and rough forage. It is small in size, with animals weighing around 600 pounds, and its dairy production is well suited to household production of milk, butter, and cheese. The breed is globally rare, though it is increasing in numbers as a result of good marketing and organization by the Irish, British, American, and Canadian breed associations. The increasing popularity of the Dexter should make agriculture analysts ponder the reasons for relative breed popularity. Dexter breeders are very happy with their sturdy, small cattle even in an agricultural environment that heavily discounts their size and production.

The Red Poll retains its dual purpose designation in Britain, but has been selected for beef in North America. This has come so recently, however, that the cows still milk well. The abundant milk supply means that the easily delivered small calves catch up to other breeds by the time they are weaned. Because Red Polls have not been widely included in the beef industry until recently, they produce strong hybrid vigor in crossbred cattle operations.

Trends in the Cattle Industry

European agricultural trends may provide a model for industry changes in North America. Milk quotas are causing many European dairy producers to reconsider the economics of the high input/high output Holstein-Friesians in favor of traditional dairy or dual purpose breeds. These traditional breeds produce moderate amounts of milk which fall within the quota levels. High forage diets and other reduced production expenses produce this milk at a lower cost than with higher input systems. The resulting beef carcass is of a much improved quality, bringing a better price than the Holstein carcass.

There are no dairy quotas in the United States, but because of the economic incentive to substitute pasture and forage for expensive grain based feeds, there is increasing interest in grass-based and seasonal dairying. A shift to more sustainable agriculture will provide a significant niche for the dual purpose breeds and a more diverse array of dairy breeds in North American agriculture.

The beef industry has recently retreated somewhat from its quest for ever larger animals as reproductive and calving problems have diminished the value of oversized animals. High birth weight calves are less economical to raise than smaller, more easily born calves which can catch up to heavier calves by weaning time. And the interval between calves is demonstrably longer in large breeds. Still, the show ring tends to award prizes to the biggest as the best, so there is conflict between the actual and perceived needs of the industry.

The American Livestock Breeds Conservancy works to conserve historic breeds not only for their aesthetic value but because of the real market resource of genetic diversity. The story of the Texas Longhorn is an excellent example of the market value of genetic conservation.

The Longhorn was developed over centuries in the arid climate of the Southwest, shaped more by natural than human selection. In the late nineteenth century, the breed was abandoned by commercial cattle producers. It nearly became extinct at the turn of the century, because railroads rendered trail hardiness unnecessary, and the breed's long horns were a packing problem in loading cattle cars for market. Except for those kept by a few stubborn ranchers, and those maintained on two federal wildlife refuges, there were few animals available when the attributes of hardiness, longevity, and strong maternal traits were rediscovered by the cattle industry. It is interesting to note that North America's best known cattle breed was not represented by a breed association until 1964 and even more interesting to see the huge increase in registrations since 1970.

The Spanish foundation stock from which the Texas Longhorn descended also produced the Florida Cracker and Pineywoods cattle of the Southeast. These breeds were shaped by the natural selection of a very different environment, and their hardiness in a hot and humid climate made them the only basis for the early Florida beef industry. In the 1930s, imported Zebu cattle were crossbred to Florida Crackers, resulting in a beef carcass with a larger size and more market appeal than either parent breed while retaining the resistance to heat, humidity, and parasites. So successful was this cross that purebred Cracker cattle nearly disappeared. With assistance of the Florida Department of Agriculture and American Livestock Breeds Conservancy, a breed association has been formed and conservation efforts are raising breed recognition and appreciation.

African breeds have also attracted some interest in North America for the genetic diversity they contain. These hardy, heat tolerant breeds are intermediate between the European breeds and the Zebu cattle. They generally lack the big ears, loose skin and humps that characterize the Indian Zebus, and they produce a carcass of more value to the processors. The N'dama breed was crossed with the Red Poll to develop the Senepol breed, while the Barzona was developed from Afrikander crossed with Hereford. Ankole Watusi from eastern Africa are being kept as purebreds as well as being used in commercial crossbreeding beef operations.

The North American cattle industry was built from a wide base of international breeds; however, import restrictions have now stopped virtually all importation of genetic stocks from Europe. This is largely due to health restrictions implemented to protect the health of our cattle population. Disease problems have continued to restrict importations from Africa, Asia, and Latin America. The effect of these restrictions has been to increase the need for maintaining our North American cattle genetic resources, which are rich indeed.

Table 8.1
Cattle Registrations

The data in this table are arranged in alphabetical order by breed. Information includes registration numbers from 1990, 1985, and 1970. Since calves are usually registered in the year of their birth, these three dates can be used to define population trends in each breed. The founding date of the association is important to determine how long the breed has had a formal support group in North America.

Breed	Number of Registrations 1990	1985	1970	Date Association Founded	Data Source[1]
American White Park	357	344		1975	t
Angus	143,520	174,539	346,195	1883	p
Canada	14,418	11,172	17,867	1906	p
Ankole Watusi	27	94		1983	s
Ayrshire	9,539	11,450	15,069	1875	p, s
Canada	9,900	14,900	10,229	1889	p
Barzona	1,300	1,000		1968	t
Beefmaster	36,458	32,100	2,800	1961	p, t
Belgian Blue	200			1988	t
Canada	75			1986	p
Belted Galloway	375	80		1951	s
Blonde D'Aquitaine	1,000			1986	t
Brahman	16,454	30,000	18,219	1924	p
Brangus	32,070	31,031	8,238	1949	p
Braunvieh	650			1984	t
British White	2,500			1987	s, t
Brown Swiss	12,473	11,974	13,743	1880	s
Canada	1,256	935	741	1901	p
Canadienne – Canada	74	411	900	1886	p
Charolais	44,725	30,000	158,000	1957	s
Chianina	8,022	21,000		1972	p, t
Canada	55	176		1972	p
Devon	177	400	858	1918	t
Dexter	500	250	75	1912	p, s, t
Canada	120			1987	p
Dutch Belted	50	100	72	1880	t
Florida Cracker	600			1989	t
Galloway	102	85	3,144	1882	s
Canada	243	265	599	1882	p
Gelbvieh	21,509	16,086		1971	p
Guernsey	18,007	25,900	43,783	1877	s
Canada	923	1,901	3,465	1905	p, s
Hays Converter – Canada	258	124		1975	p
Hereford (Horned)	97,424	120,000	253,832	1881	p
Canada (Horned/Polled)	35,045	42,975	59,499	1890	t

Herens	12	5		1980	t
Highland	766	518	516	1948	p, t
Canada	437	177	124	1964	p
Holstein	380,009	394,506	281,574	1885	p, t
Canada	159,112	149,014	98,800	1884	t
Jersey	53,709	50,000	37,800	1868	p
Canada	7,001	7,978	7,383	1901	p
Kerry	4				p
Canada	16	4		1992	t
Limousin	59,074	44,484		1968	p
Lineback	200			1985	p
Luing – Canada	8	26		1975	p
Maine-Anjou	8,000	3,400		1969	t
Marchigiana	66	432		1973	s
Milking Devon	120	15		1978	t
Milking Shorthorn	3,524	3,374	4,263	1944	p
Murray Grey	900	500		1970	p
Canada	302	343		1970	p
Normande	350	350		1974	t
Piedmontese	783			1984	t
Canada	195	10		1901	p
Pineywoods	300[a]				t
Pinzgauer	997	1,000	1,320	1973	t
Polled Hereford	72,113	96,456	168,021	1901	p, t
Randall Lineback	30[a]				t
Red Angus	15,353	12,482	8,512	1954	s
Canada	7,746	3,416			p
Red Poll	1,432	1,472	1,777	1883	p
Canada	262	113	206	1905	p
Romagnola	400			1976	t
Salers	21,464	12,506		1974	p
Canada	1,489			1974	p
Santa Gertrudis	6,050	28,000	16,837	1951	p
Senepol	1,480				p, s, t
Shorthorn	8,002	16,662	35,653	1846	p
Canada	3,217	2,636		1886	p
Simmental	90,516	85,533		1969	p
South Devon	1,700	2,500		1974	t
Canada	101	45		1974	p
Sussex	0			1890	t
Tarentaise	1,500	2,949		1973	p, s
Canada	410	200		1973	p
Texas Longhorn	12,373	8,509	500	1964	p
Welsh Black	1,000	200		1975	p, t
White Park	14			1991	p, t
Zebu	1,000	5,000		1946	t

[1] p = published information; s = survey; t = telephone interview
[a] No registry exists for this breed or the registry data are not complete. This is an estimate of the purebreds born in North America.

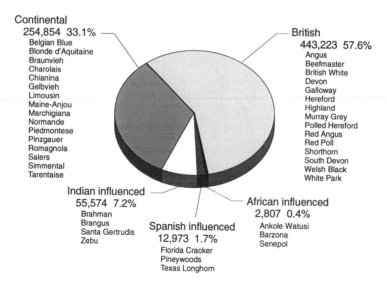

Figure 8.2. North American beef cattle breeds — 1990 registrations by geographic origin.

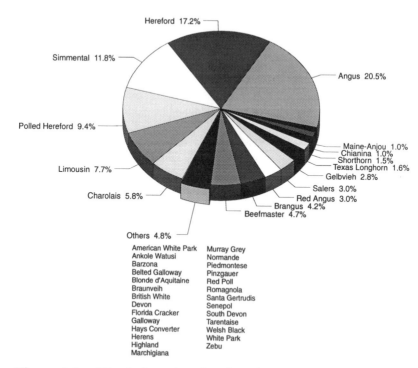

Figure 8.3. North American beef cattle breeds — comparison of purebred registrations for 1990.

46

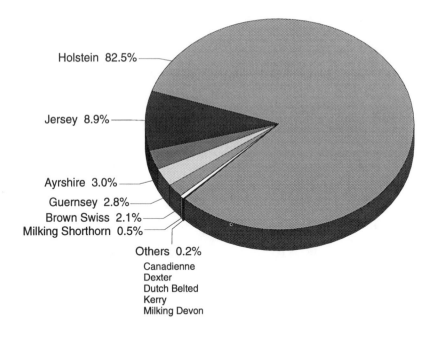

Holstein 82.5%

Jersey 8.9%

Ayrshire 3.0%

Guernsey 2.8%

Brown Swiss 2.1%

Milking Shorthorn 0.5%

Others 0.2%
Canadienne
Dexter
Dutch Belted
Kerry
Milking Devon

Figure 8.4. North American dairy cattle breeds —
a comparison of purebred registrations for 1990.

Conservation Priority Cattle Breeds

Critical: Fewer than 200 annual registrations in North America and an estimated global population of less than 2,000.

Ankole Watusi
Devon
Dutch Belted
Florida Cracker *
Herens
Kerry
Milking Devon *
Pineywoods *
Randall Lineback *
White Park

Rare: Fewer than 1,000 annual registrations in North America and an estimated global population of less than 5,000.

Belted Galloway
Canadienne *
Dexter
Galloway

Watch: Fewer than 2,500 annual registrations in North America and an estimated global population of less than 10,000. Also included are dairy cattle breeds which are above numerical guidelines but show a marked decline in numbers over the last 20 years.

Ayrshire
British White
Guernsey
Highland
Milking Shorthorn
Red Poll
Senepol *

* Unique to North America

Several breeds which are low in numbers have not been included on the ALBC priority list. The Hays Converter and Luing were not included since they could theoretically be reconstituted from their numerically strong foundation breeds. Breeds with open herd books, such as the American Lineback, are also not included, since they do not represent a true breed in the genetic sense. The American White Park is a recently developed breed which is differentiated from the White Park by outcrosses with British White, Shorthorn, and perhaps other breeds. Many European breeds of recent import are rare in North America but are globally numerous. This is also true of the Murray Grey, which is of Australian origin.

Cattle Breed Associations

American White Park Cattle Association of America, 419 N Water St, Madrid, IA 50156; Joyce Fisher, 515-795-2013.

American **Angus** Association, 3201 Frederick Blvd, St Joseph, MO 64501; Richard L. Spader, 816-233-3101.

Canadian Aberdeen **Angus** Association, Box 3209, Regina, SK S4P 3H1, Canada; John Willmott, 306-757-6885.

Ankole Watusi International Registry, RR 1 Box 97, Spring Hill, KS 66038; Elizabeth Lundgren, 913-686-3271.

World **Watusi** Association, HC 77 Box 66, Crawford, NE 69339; Maureen Neidhart, 308-665-1321.

Ayrshire Breeders Association, PO Box 1608, Brattleboro, VT 05302-1608; 802-254-7460.

Ayrshire Breeders Association of Canada, 1160 Carling Ave, Ottawa, ON K1Z 7K6, Canada, Joyce Trafford.

Barzona Breeders Association of America, PO Box 631, Prescott, AZ 86302; Karen Halford ,602-445-5150.

Beefmaster Breeders Universal, 6800 Park Ten Blvd, San Antonio, TX 78213; Gene Kuykendall, 512-732-3132.

American **Belgian Blue** Association, PO Box 307, City Springs, TX 75482-0307; Phil Myers, Executive Director, 903-885-2275.

Canadian **Belgian Blue** Association, RR 1, Inglewood, ON L0N 1K0, Canada; Joanne Currie, 416-838-2844.

Belted Galloway Society, 7118 Elliott Ln, Leeds, AL 35094; Mary C. McClellan, 205-699-8938.

American **Blonde D'Aquitaine** Association, PO Box 1234, Kansas City, MO 64116; 816-421-1305.

American **Brahman** Breeders Association, 1313 La Concha Ln, Houston, TX 77054; Wendell Schronk, 713-795-4444.

International **Brangus** Assciation, PO Box 696020, San Antonio, TX 78269-6020; J. Neil Orth, 512-696-8231.

Braunvieh Association of America, PO Box 6396, Lincoln, NE 68506; Iola Doeschot, 402-421-2960.

British White Cattle Association of America, RR 10 Box 67, West Des Moines, IA 50265; Tom Zimmerman, 515-225-1136.

Brown Swiss Association, USA, PO Box 1038, Beloit, WI 53511-1038; George Harris, 608-365-4474.

Canadian **Brown Swiss** Association, 350 Speedvale W #9, Guelf, ON N1H 7M7, Canada; Diana MacDonald, 519-821-2811.

Canadienne Cattle Breeders Association, 211-12E Sud, Apt 2, Sherbrooke, PQ J1G 2V5, Canada; Jean-Guy Bernier, 819-567-1258.

American International **Charolais** Association, PO Box 20247, Kansas City, MO 64195; Joe Garrett, 816-464-5977.

American **Chianina** Association, PO Box 890, Platte City, MO 64079; Robert Vantrease, 816-431-2808.

Canadian **Chianina** Association, c/o Mabel Sharp, General Delivery, Coalhurst, AB T0L 0V0, Canada.

North American **Corriente** Association, 9101 E. Kenyon Ave, Suite 3000, Denver, CO 80237; 303-770-0144.

Devon Cattle Association, Inc., PO Box 17090, Tucson, AZ 85731-7090; Stewart Fowler, 602-751-1320.

American **Dexter** Cattle Association, RR 1 Box 378, Concordia, MO 64020; Rosemary Fleharty, 816-463-7704.

Canadian **Dexter** Cattle Association, RR 1, Keene, ON K0L 2G0, Canada; Winona Crapp, 705-295-6536.

Dutch Belted Association of America, c/o American Livestock Breeds Conservancy, PO Box 477, Pittsboro, NC 27312; Don Bixby, 919-542-5704.

Florida Cracker Cattle Association, Mayo Building, Rm 425, Tallahasee, FL 32399-0860.

American **Galloway** Breeders Association, RR 6 Box 140, Elkhorn, WI 53121; Zoe Siperly, 414-723-3276.

Canadian **Galloway** Association, RR 1, Puslinch, ON N0B 2J0, Canada; Dawn VanKampen, 519-821-7493.

American **Gelbvieh** Association, 10900 Dover St, Westminster, CO 80021; Dr. James B. Gibb, 303-465-2333.

American **Guernsey** Cattle Club, PO Box 666, Reynoldsburg, OH 43068-0666; Neil Jensen, 614-864-2409.

Canadian **Guernsey** Association, 368 Woolwich St, Guelph, ON N1H 3W6, Canada; Vivianne MacDonald, 519-836-2141.

Canadian **Hays Converter** Association, 310, 4723 1st St SW, Calgary, AB T2G 4YB, Canada; Sidney B. Williams, 403-243-1186.

American **Hereford** Association, 1501 Wyandotte, Kansas City, MO 64101; H H Dickenson, 816-842-3757.

Canadian **Hereford** Association, 5160 Skyline Way NE, Calgary, AB T2E 6V1, Canada; Duncan J. Panteous, Secretary/General Manager, 403-275-2662.

American **Herens** Cattle Association, PO Box 1250, Lewisburg, WV 24901; George Lemon, 304-645-3773.

American **Highland** Cattle Association, PO Box 81, Remer, MN 56672; Francine Hogate, 218-566-1321.

Canadian **Highland** Cattle Society, 58 Bailey Rd, RR1, Knowlton, PQ J0E 1VO, Canada; Margaret Badger, 514-243-5543.

Holstein Association, 1 Holstein Pl, Brattleboro, VT 05301-0808; Thomas J. Moses, 802-254-4551.

Holstein Association of Canada, PO Box 610, Brantford, ON N3T 5R4, Canada; David Clemons, 519-756-8300.

American **Jersey** Cattle Club, 6486 E Main St, Reynoldsburg, OH 43068; Erick Metzger, 614-861-3636.

Jersey Cattle Association of Canada, 350 Speedvale W #9, Guelph, ON N1H 7M7, Canada; Russell G. Gammon, 519-821-1020.

North American **Kerry** Cattle Association, c/o Joywind Farm Rare Breeds Conservancy, Inc, General Delivery, Marmora, ON K0K 2M0, Canada; Jy Chiperzak, 613-472-6160.

North American **Limousin** Foundation, PO Box 4467, Englewood, CO 80155; John W. Edwards, 303-220-1693.

American **Lineback** Registry, Daniels Farm Rd, Irasburg, VT 05845; Paul Daniels, 802-755-6105.

Canadian **Luing** Cattle Association, c/o Mrs. Richard J. Luft, Kathyrn, AB T0M 1E0, Canada; 403-935-4414.

American **Maine-Anjou** Association, 528 Livestock Exchange Building, 1600 Genesee St, Suite 567, Kansas City, MO 64102-1008; John Boddicker, 816-474-9555.

American International **Marchigiana** Society, Box 198, Walton, KS 67151; Martie Knudsen, 316-837-3303.

Canadian **Meuse-Rhine-Ijssel** Association, Box 235, Claresholm, AB T0L 0T0, Canada; Mrs. J. Lozeman, 403-625-4516.

American **Milking Devon** Association, PO Box 730, New Durham, NH 03855; Sue Randall, 603-859-6611.

American **Milking Shorthorn** Society, PO Box 449, Beloit, WI 53511-0449; Wendy Gimler, 608-365-3332.

American **Murray Grey** Association, PO Box 30085, Billings, MT 59101; Joan L. Turnquist, 406-248-1266.

Canadian **Murray Grey** Association, Box 605, Red Deer, AB T4N 5G6, Canada; Doris Burrington, 403-343-1355.

North American **Normande** Association, RR 1 Box 7, Hanlontown, IA 50444; Craig Ouveron, 515-896-2601.

Piedmontese Association of the U.S., Livestock Exchange #108, Denver, CO 80216; Mary Jo McCormick, 303-295-7287.

Canadian **Piedmontese** Association, Box 605, Red Deer, AB T4N 5G6, Canada; Doris Burrington, 403-347-2788.

Pineywoods, c/o American Livestock Breeds Conservancy, PO Box 477, Pittsboro, NC 27312; 919-542-5704.

American **Pinzgauer** Association, 21555 State Rd 698, Jenera, OH 45841; Peg Meents, 419-326-8711.

American **Polled Hereford** Association, 11020 NW Ambassador Dr, Kansas City, MO 64153-2034; 816-891-8400.

Randall Lineback, c/o American Livestock Breeds Conservancy, PO Box 477, Pittsboro, NC 27312; 919-542-5704.

Red Angus Association of America, 4201 N Interstate 35, Denton, TX 76207-3496; Dr. Richard Gilbert, 817-387-3502.

American **Red Poll** Association, PO Box 35519, Louisville, KY 40232; Carrie Schueler, 502-635-6540.

Canadian **Red Poll** Association, RR 3, Ponoka, AB T0C 2H0, Canada; Jackie Fleming, 403-783-5951.

American **Romagnola** Association, PO Box 450, Navasota, TX 77868; Sandra Wright, 409-825-8082.

American **Salers** Association, 5600 S Quebec #200, Englewood, CO 80111; Robert Rolston, 303-770-9292.

Salers Association of Canada, Rm 228, 2116 27th Ave, Calgary, AB T2E 7A6, Canada; Neil Majeski, 403-291-2620.

Santa Gertrudis Breeders International, PO Box 1257, Kingsville, TX 78364; Jim Reeves, 512-592-9357.

North American **Senepol** Association, PO Box 901594, Kansas City, MO 64190-1594; Mike Todd, 1-800-SENEPOL.

American **Shorthorn** Association, 8288 Hascall St, Omaha, NE 68124; Dr. Roger Hunsley, 402-393-7200.

Canadian **Shorthorn** Association, 5 Douglas St, Guelph, ON N1H 2S8, Canada; Patricia Coulson, 519-822-6841.

American **Simmental** Association, 1 Simmental Way, Bozeman, MT 59715; Brian G. Kitchen, 800-548-0205.

North American **South Devon** Association, PO Box 68, Lynnville, IA 50153; Dr. T. E. Fitzpatrick, 515-527-2437.

Canadian **South Devon** Association, Box 667, Olds, AB T0M 1P0, Canada; Lesley Fischer, 405-556-6900.

Sussex Cattle Association of America, PO Box 107, Refugio, TX 78377; Lawrence Wood, 512-526-2380.

American **Tarentaise** Association, PO Box 34705, North Kansas City, MO 64116; James Spawn, 816-421-1993.

Canadian **Tarentaise** Association, Box 333, Aberdeen, SK S0K 0A0, Canada; Bridget Hamoline, 306-253-4443.

Texas Longhorn Breeders Association, PO Box 4430, Fort Worth, TX 76106; Russel Harriman, 817-625-6241.

Welsh Black Association, USA, RR 1 Box 76B, Shelburn, IN 47879; Sue Case, 812-383-9233.

North American **White Park** Cattle Association, HC 87 Box 2214, Big Timber, MT 59011; Wes Henthorne, 409-932-4197.

International **Zebu** Breeders Association, PO Box 757, Kyle, TX 78640; Janie Smith, 512-268-0950.

Other Resources

National Cattlemen's Association, PO Box 3469, Englewood, CO 80155; 303-694-0305, and state cattlemen's associations.

Purebred Dairy Cattle Association, Inc., Bradford Ellsworth, Secretary, PO Box 160, Cabool, MO 65689; 417-962-3141.

Chapter 9

Goats

The domestic goat may be our true best friend because of the services it has long rendered to humankind. Goats, derived from several species of the genus *Capra*, have provided meat, milk, and fiber, all the while prospering on marginal land. Their browsing and foraging abilities, which complement the grazing habits of other livestock species, are put to good use clearing brush and maintaining a diversified grassland. The goat's sociable personality makes it a good companion for people and other animals alike.

Figure 9.1. San Clemente goats.

Maurice Shelton of the Texas Agricultural Experiment Station estimates there may be five to ten million goats in the United States today. The many goat breeds and types found in North America are derived from importations of European, Asian, and African breeds. Of the six dairy breeds in North America, four — the Alpine, Oberhasli, Saanen, and Toggenburg — are of Swiss or northern European origin. Other dairy goats are the Nubian, developed in England from Indian and African stocks, and the LaMancha, a recently established American breed of Spanish origin. The Angora, the most popular fiber producing goat, was imported to North America from Turkey. Nigerian Dwarf and Pygmy goats are companion breeds of African origin. North Americans enjoy a wealth of diversity in these distinct breeds, and each one serves an invaluable purpose in the agricultural picture.

Current import restrictions prohibit restocking populations in the United States from anywhere except Australia and New Zealand. The cost, time, and other risks involved deter most breeders from this route, and in any event the breeds available in Australia and New Zealand are very limited. The populations that currently exist in North America should therefore be monitored carefully for changes.

Dairy Goats

Six breeds dominate the dairy goat industry: Alpine, LaMancha, Nubian, Oberhasli, Saanen, and Toggenburg. While some breeders are raising dairy goats for commercial use, many more keep them for small scale production or as a hobby. The Nigerian Dwarf goat is sometimes milked, though because of its small size it generally produces only enough milk for home consumption.

In most states there are stringent regulations for the sale of raw milk. These health regulations require inspection and certification of facilities and production processes before milk can be sold from the farm, limiting the options of producers with small herds. As a result, many breeders direct their breeding programs toward the show ring as well as dairy production.

The Nubian goat is especially pertinent to a discussion of breed and genetic resources. Of all the dairy breeds in North America, the Nubian has the most pronounced dual purpose qualities. This was especially so in the past, but is decreasing as selection is now molding the breed into the conformation favored for the Swiss breeds. The Nubian still possesses characteristics which make it an excellent candidate for dual purpose use, such as aseasonal reproduction, large frame, and large litter size.

Fiber Goats

The fibers produced by goats — mohair and cashmere — are known around the world for their luxury and utility. Mohair is produced by Angora goats. (Angora fiber is produced by Angora rabbits.) Cashmere is not a breed name, but rather the term for the downy undercoat produced by many goats in variable amounts and qualities.

Angora goats first arrived in North America in 1849. They gradually spread throughout the United States, but the population was nearly eliminated during the Civil War. Subsequent importations increased their numbers so that today the state of Texas not only has the largest concentration of Angora goats in North America, but is the second largest producer of mohair in the world.

Mohair is known for its softness, beauty, and strength, as well as the high market price it commands as a finished product. Even though North America is second in mohair production, the industrial infrastructure does not exist in North America for mohair processing; ninety percent of the fiber is processed abroad. The United States then imports about twenty percent of the world's finished mohair products.

There are two breed organizations which promote and register Angora goats. The American Angora Goat Breeders' Association Registry maintains a closed herd book, which means that undocumented animals, even if purebred, may not be registered. The Angora Goat Record and Registry of North America was formed in 1985 as a genetic recovery program to register upgraded or partially documented animals. Since only a small number of purebred Angora goats are registered annually, the American Angora Goat Breeders' Association Registry declined to release registration figures for this census, feeling that publishing this figure would misrepresent the number in the total breed population. Therefore the figures in this census reflect only those upgraded Angora goats that are registered with the Angora Goat Record and Registry of North America.

Cashmere goats are not a true genetic breed and there is no registry for goats that produce cashmere. The cashmere fiber (also known as pashmina) is the winter undercoat of the goat, and it is not produced exclusively by a specific breed. Rather, any goat may have cashmere characteristics. The heritability of cashmere is not well understood and this limits its availability.

Importations from Australia and New Zealand have increased the availability of cashmere producing goats in North America. Demand by spinners and weavers has fueled increasing interest in this fiber. Much of the current cashmere production is processed and used outside the usual commercial channels, and these trends will likely continue.

The Pygora goat is a relatively new breed developed by crossing Pygmy and Angora goats. The registry accepts animals whose parents are registered with either the American Angora Breeders' Association or the National Pygmy Goat Association. The breed produces two distinct coats, an inner hair similar to cashmere and an outer fleece which is mohair.

Meat Goats

Since goats are able to thrive under a variety of conditions with relatively low input, they are a major source of meat worldwide. Even goats raised for other purposes are ultimately used as a source of meat, which is known as chevon.

Although chevon is a common and preferred meat in many cultures, it is relatively unfamiliar to North Americans. One important quality of chevon is its low fat and cholesterol content. Growing ethnic markets provide increasing opportunities for year round sales of goat meat, in contrast to the previously seasonal peak during spring religious celebrations. Although the industry has not developed a system for processing and marketing goat meat, independent producers are becoming more adept at marketing their own product. They are selling chevon to specialty restaurants and gourmet stores that have an ethnic clientele and cater to the growing public interest in the foods of other cultures.

No breed of goat in North America is specified as a meat goat. The market is primarily based on culled dairy and fiber animals. In spite of this situation, there are some breeds in North America that fit better than others into the category of meat goat. One of these is the Pygmy goat. It has the advantages of aseasonal reproduction, multiple births, and good meat conformation. The Pygmy is currently being used in crossbreeding programs for meat production in Canada. Its small size limits its widespread acceptance as a meat goat, however, as does public perception of the Pygmy as a companion rather than as a meat animal.

The Kinder goat is a new breed that was developed by crossing the Pygmy and Nubian. Breeders of this goat hope to secure the attributes of each of these breeds in one animal, a dual purpose goat used both for its meat and milk production.

The Tennessee Fainting and Wooden Leg are myotonic goats which have been used historically as a source of meat. Myotonic goats have a muscular abnormality that causes them to stiffen when startled. These goats are currently being standardized as small novelty animals, but their potential as an improved meat goat is being largely overlooked. Aseasonal reproduction, multiple births, and stocky conformation make them ideal choices for consideration as meat animals.

The Spanish goat is another breed type with potential for meat production in North America. The pure Spanish goat is a unique genetic resource that descended from goats brought by Spanish explorers and colonists to the New World. This historic type no longer exists in Spain, therefore the American Spanish goat is its closest modern representative. The best-documented Spanish populations are the goats of San Clemente Island (California) and Mona Island (Puerto Rico), though Spanish goats are found throughout the Caribbean and the southern United States.

A handicap to the use and conservation of the Spanish goat is the confusion over its name, which is used to describe both purebred and crossbred animals in the Southwest. Spanish goats in the Southeast are generally referred to as Brush goats, though this term is also often used to describe animals of unknown breeding. Improved documentation of the Spanish goat breed group and an expanded market niche as a meat animal would aid in its conservation.

The Multipurpose Goat

Goats are excellent browsers and can be useful in land management programs. They consume brush, shrubs, and other plants in preference to grass. For that reason, goats can appropriately share pasture space with other ruminants. They can also be used to eat rapidly growing pest plants such as blackberry, kudzu, multiflora rose, poison ivy, and other tenacious woody invaders, thereby allowing natural plant diversity to return. Browsing interrupts regrowth in general, keeps land open for other uses, and can be used to encourage selective reforestation of certain desired plant species. Goats must be managed carefully, however, since they can eat vegetation down to the point of obliteration.

Goats can also be used for recreation and as personable companions. Cart goats were especially popular in the early part of the century. Goats can serve as pack animals since they are able to scale steep trails in mountains carrying packs of up to one hundred pounds. Goats in the Northwest were used during the Klondike gold expeditions from 1897 to 1899. They were able to withstand the bitter cold and the dangerous trek up the mountain trails while serving their owners by hauling food and equipment. Pack goat proponents say that the environmental impact of goats is far less than that of other pack animals, particularly horses.

Trends

The American Dairy Goat Association registration numbers reached a peak in the early 1980s, followed by a reduction in numbers from 1982 through 1990, and a gradual increase since then. Even the Oberhasli, the dairy breed with the lowest registration numbers, has seen an increase in registrations between 1990 and 1992.

The current market for dairy goat products is relatively small but growing as people become acquainted with the taste of goat milk and cheeses. Some people allergic to cows' milk are able to tolerate the milk of goats. The market for goat cheese is increasing steadily and fewer processing restrictions apply to cheese than to fluid milk. As a result, goat cheeses are finding their way into restaurants and specialty markets.

The goat industry as a whole, however, faces several obstacles in its attempt to promote a wide variety of goat breeds. One problem is a suspected high rate of turnover among goat breeders. People may be attracted to raising goats as pets or for market to make a quick profit, but marketing goat products is a challenge not met by short term interest. Rapid turnover means that long term, well considered breeding programs are the exception rather than the rule.

Another problem is the lack of consumer awareness. Goat meat, dairy products, and fiber are still unfamiliar to much of the North American population, and goat production and marketing function primarily through cottage industries which lack the infrastructure for expansion. Shared expertise in the production, processing, and marketing of meat goats is not readily available to new producers. This is beginning to change, however, with the organization of producer networks, such as the Florida Meat Goat Association, established to encourage the production and marketing of a product which is in direct competition with chicken, beef, and pork. The marketing of dairy products is better supported through the efforts of the American Dairy Goat Association which provides technical and marketing advice to dairy producers.

A third problem facing the goat industry is the lack of attention given to specific pure breeds. Growth in the goat industry has kept most of the breeds numerically strong, but there are many goat populations that are not registered and therefore are not accurately counted. This is especially true of the Spanish and Angora breeds. It is difficult to determine what has been lost genetically if it is not known what was there in the first place. Documentation of breeds allows for a better understanding of the parameters of each breed as well as for maintaining the distinctiveness of the various breeds.

Despite these obstacles, the use of goats in agricultural settings is increasing. The growing interest has generated research on goats, as evidenced by the North Carolina State University Cooperative Extension Service 1992 publication *North Carolina Meat Goat Handbook*. This handbook contains research papers from Florida A & M University, University of California at Davis, Texas A & M University, University of Florida, and the E. (Kika) de la Garza Institute for Goat Research, Langston University in Oklahoma. Publications like this *Handbook* are excellent resources for goat breeders.

Conservation Priorities

A top priority is the genetic evaluation of the Spanish and Brush goat populations of the southwestern and southeastern United States. These goats are not well defined genetically, yet they may include unique populations that are globally significant. No registries or associations for these breeds exist.

The myotonic breeds, Tennessee Fainting and Texas Wooden Leg, are also in need of additional genetic documentation. These breeds represent historic landrace populations which have better defined genetic parameters than earlier assumed. Initial evaluation of the history and phenotype of the Wooden Leg indicates that the breed is derived from Tennessee stock. These breeds are closely related if not in fact two parts of the same breed. Some populations of Fainting goats have been selected (and crossbred) as a miniature novelty for the exotic animal market. This practice is detrimental to the genetic documentation, promotion, and conservation of Tennessee Fainting goats, which are a unique genetic resource.

More research on these goat breeds is of particular urgency given the changes expected in the North American meat goat market. The Boer goat, a large framed South African meat breed recently imported from New Zealand, is expected to have a significant impact on meat goat breeding in North America. It is likely that American meat goats will be crossbred with Boer goats to increase carcass size, and native stocks will be lost.

Table 9.1
Goat Registrations

The American Dairy Goat Association was especially forthcoming with census information about each of the dairy goat breeds. An annual count of registration figures for each breed after 1985 suggests the growth patterns of dairy breeds in North America.

For some of the breeds, including the Tennessee Fainting goat, more than one registry exists. In these cases it is not always clear what part of the registration figures represent animals registered in both groups. Such figures are coded as estimates.

It was extremely difficult to gather accurate breed registration figures for some of the other goat breeds. Even when registries do exist, figures are not always available. For example, although the Angora goat has a global population in the millions, very few of the animals are registered. Registration figures from the National Pygmy Goat Association were not made available to ALBC for this census, although the Pygmy is a widely recognized and popular breed with a sophisticated structure for competitive showing.

Breed	Number of Registrations 1990	1985	Data Source[1]
Alpine	8,343		t
Canada	20	862	p
Angora	581[a]		t
Canada	800	503	p
Brush	No registry exists		
Cashmere	No registry exists		
Kinder	121		s
LaMancha	3,659		t
Canada	90	50	p
Nigerian Dwarf	1,512[b]	179	t
Canada	53	0	p
Nubian	14,364		t
Canada	997	922	p
Oberhasli	1,108		t
Canada	1	0	p
Pygmy	Data unavailable		t
Canada	112	68	p
Pygora	350		s
Saanen	3,742		t
Canada	267	366	p
San Clemente	100[b]		p, t
Spanish	No registry exists		
Tennessee Fainting	950[b]		t

Toggenburg	3,138		t
Canada	275	534	p
Wooden Leg	No registry exists		t

[1] p = published information; s = survey; t = telephone interview.
[a] Figure is from one of the two registries and represents only a fraction of the total Angora population.
[b] Estimate

Conservation Priority Goat Breeds

Critical: Fewer than 200 annual registrations in North America and an estimated global population of less than 2,000.

San Clemente (F)*

Rare: Fewer than 1,000 annual registrations in North America and an estimated global population of less than 5,000.

Nigerian Dwarf

Watch: Fewer than 2,500 annual registrations in North America and an estimated global population of less than 10,000.

Oberhasli

Study: Populations of genetic interest which lack breed definition or documentation.
Brush *
Spanish *
Tennessee Fainting *
Wooden Leg *

* = Unique to North America
(F) = Feral population or breed of feral origin

Despite their relatively small numbers, the Kinder and Pygora goats are not listed as conservation priorities. These are newly developed breeds, which could be recreated from their numerically strong foundation breeds.

Goats Breed Associations

(The date in parenthesis is the year the association was founded).

American **Goat** Society (1934), RR 1 Box 56, Esperance, NY 12066; John Howland, 518-875-6708.

Canadian **Goat** Society (1917), PO Box 357, 4098 St Andrews W, Fergus, ON N1M 3E2 Canada; 519-843-3294.

American **Dairy Goat** Association (1904), PO Box 865, Spindale, NC 28160; Keith Maxey, 704-286-3801.

International **Dairy Goat** Registry (1980), PO Box 309, Chickamauga, GA 30707; Robert Johnson, 404-375-4326.

American **Angora** Goat Breeders' Association (1900), PO Box 195, Rocksprings, TX 78880; 512-683-4483.

Angora Goat Record & Registry of North America (1985), 1451 Sisson Rd., Freeport, MI 49325; Sue Drummond, 616-765-3056.

International **Fainting** Goat Association (1990), Registrar, 3450 230th St, Terril, IA 51364; Ruth Prentice, 712-853-6372.

Mohair Council of America (1969), PO Box 5337, San Angelo, TX 76902; Brian May, 915-655-3161.

Cashmere Producers of America, PO Box 27, Virginia Dale, CO 80548; 303-493-6015.

Kinder Goat Breeders' Association (1988), 16212 Bothell-Everett Hwy, Mill Creek, WA 98012; Teresa Hill, President, 206-668-5136.Breed Associations

Nigerian Dwarf Goat Foundation, c/o Kathy Claps, RR 1 Box 368, Red Rock, TX 78662.

National **Pygmy** Goat Association (1975), 166 Blackstone St, Mendon, MA 01756; Terry Pleau, General Manager, 508-478-5902.

Pygora Breeders' Association (1987), 16619 S Bradley Rd, Oregon City, OR 97045; Katherine Jorgensen.

American **Tennessee Fainting** Goat Association (1988), RR 3 Box 61, Minden, NE 68959; Todd L. Petersen, 308-237-9338.

Chapter 10

Horses

Horses (*Equus caballus*) are part of the service sector of agriculture and greater society, being used extensively for recreation, sport, draft power, and transportation, and only secondarily for food. Horses work closely with people and much of the worth of an individual animal may come from the value added by training.

Not surprisingly, the breeding of horses historically has been directed toward goals relevant to use and personal preference, including athletic ability, color, gaits, size, and style. As a result, there is a

Figure 10.1. Spanish Mustang horses.

great and easily recognized variety of breeds, but they are particularly vulnerable to economic and social changes. The twentieth century has been a time of such changes. Horses reached their maximum numbers in North America in the early 1900s and then declined dramatically when animal power was replaced by the machine power of tractors, trucks, and trains. Since World War II, the primary area of growth in the use of horses has been in sport and recreation.

Three trends have emerged to dominate modern horse breeding: the changing selection within breeds, which may converge even originally distinct breeds around a common type; the alteration of breeds through crossbreeding, which accelerates the convergence of horse types; and the emphasis on athletic performance, with less attention to overall soundness.

Selection within breeds has changed in response to the markets available. Generally, markets for horses have become more specialized and more limited since World War II. For example, the demand for working draft horses has declined relative to the market for show and hitch horses. As a result, the draft breeds have generally been selected for greater height and flashier style, while animals of compact size (which are handier on the farm) have declined in popularity. Broad and diverse markets encourage genetic diversity; a specialized, limited market can result in genetic uniformity.

A more dramatic trend has been the alteration of breeds through crossbreeding. Since mid-century, most riding horse breeds have been changed (breeders say "improved") through the systematic introduction of Arabian, Thoroughbred, Quarter Horse, or other breeds, as a way to add refinement, size, style, and speed — traits deemed essential to meet a growing demand for sport and show horses. Regardless of intent, this type of improvement is crossbreeding, and it dilutes the genetic uniqueness of a breed. As more and more breeds are crossed with the Thoroughbred, for example, they are more like each other, and the genetic diversity available to the entire equine species is reduced.

Modern horse breeding has put great emphasis on athletic performance. This emphasis has been made at the expense of qualities necessary to working horses, such as soundness, hardiness, and adaptability. The old adage says, "no foot, no horse," but improvements in veterinary care are now readily available to allow horses to perform or at the least reproduce when they are unsound.

The Horse Industry

Horses are big business in North America. The American Horse Council estimates in its 1992 *Horse Industry Directory* that in the United States alone, horses are a $15.2 billion industry. This is approximately

83 percent of the gross national product (GNP) of the textile sector; 65 percent of the GNP of the lumber and wood products sector; or 16 percent of the GNP of the agriculture, forestry, and fisheries sector of the economy.

There are over 6.6 million horses in the United States today (1992 *Horse Industry Directory*). According to an American Horse Council study, the four most numerous breeds accounted for approximately 70 percent of the United States purebred population in 1987. The American Quarter Horse breed was the most numerous single pure-bred population, with 1.8 million horses, or 38 percent of the total. The Quarter Horse was followed by the Arabian (620,000, or 18 percent), the Thoroughbred (533,000, or 11 percent) and the Standard-bred (150,000, or 3 percent).[1] Breeds with Arabian, Quarter Horse, or Thoroughbred influence, or grades of these common breeds, make up most of the remaining population, leaving only a few breeds which are not closely related.

The horse industry in North America went through a period of expansion during the late 1970s and early 1980s. Tax policies and economic growth favored investment in horses as tangible assets, both for racing and for other recreational uses. By the mid- to late 1980s, however, the period of growth had reversed, due in part to the economic recession and in part to changes in the tax code. Horses were less attractive as investments and the recession meant fewer dollars available for recreation. By 1990, the horse industry had bottomed out and fewer total horses were registered than at any time since 1975. The Appaloosa Horse Club, for example, had registrations drop over 50 percent between 1980 and 1990. The rarer breeds were less affected by either the boom or the bust.[2]

Though the competitive businesses of racing and sport provide the fuel for growth, the backbone of the horse industry is backyard recreation. One bright spot amid economic difficulties has been the continuing strength of breed association membership figures and the numbers of transfers, which indicate that new people are being attracted to horse ownership.[3]

Draft Horses

Draft horse breeds declined precipitously with farm mechanization after World War II. The 1950s were the low point for all draft horse breeds, but a steady recovery began in the decades that followed. The draft breeds shared in horse industry growth of the early 1980s and today annual registrations for the Belgian, Clydesdale, and Percheron breed associations are at a fifty year high. The Shire and Suffolk horses, more rare in North America, are also seeing increases in the number of registrations and in breed association memberships. Though critically endangered, the American Cream Draft is also experiencing an increase in the number of horses and breeders.

There are two primary uses for draft horses. Traditional use in agriculture remains the most important. Draft horses are particularly well suited for diversified farms, where their food can be produced and their manure put to use as fertilizer. Horses serve as a sole source of power on some farms, while on others they are used instead of a second tractor. The power provided by horses (or by oxen or mules) complements the work of a tractor by working an area more slowly and thoroughly with less soil compaction. Animals are arguably superior to tractors for logging and farm work on marginal and uneven land.

A second use for draft horses is recreation, which has accounted for much of the growth in breed populations during the 1980s. This includes driving, part-time farming, and showing. While Budweiser's Clydesdales are the best known of the fancy draft horse hitches, there are now several promotional teams which carry corporate sponsorship. The power and drama of draft horses, as presented in the show ring, has raised public awareness of the draft breeds and attracted new breeders.

A third, less significant use of draft horses is crossbreeding with Thoroughbreds and other light breeds to produce medium weight riding and driving horses of good disposition and substance. The Percheron is the most widely used for this purpose, though Clydesdales and Shires are also used. Draft horse mares are also crossed with Mammoth Jacks to produce draft mules.

Ponies and Miniature Horses

Most ponies are used as children's pleasure and show mounts, with an increasing demand for jumping ponies. Breeds such as the Connemara are benefitting from this trend, especially as they become more widely known. Driving represents an opportunity for adult involvement with ponies and may have an impact on some of the rarer breeds, such as the Exmoor, Dartmoor, and Gotland.

Miniature horses have a separate market as high priced pets and investments. Horses are but one part of the market for miniature animals, which also includes goats, donkeys, and pigs.

Riding Horses

Most riding horses are used by adults for pleasure riding or for sport. Horse sports include endurance and trail riding, dressage, driving, hunting/jumping, and racing. Some of these activities call for a particular breed: flat racing, for example, is dominated by Thoroughbreds and harness racing by Standardbreds. Most performance events, however, are open to horses of any breed within a general type. For this reason, buyers of performance or pleasure horses are usually searching for a good individual of a general type rather than an animal of a specific breed. Owners of horses are not typically breeders; their interest is generally in the performance abilities of a single horse rather than its reproductive potential as part of a herd. In many cases, as long as the animal is registered, the specific breed is little more than a status symbol. As one breed secretary noted, many buyers do not appreciate the difference between a breed and a set of (registration) papers.

Given this casual view of the breed concept among horse people, it is not surprising that so many associations have chosen to open their registries for "improvement" based on crossbreeding. The result has been a greater uniformity of the entire group of riding breeds. The American Quarter Horse, for example, opened its studbook to include Thoroughbred outcrosses. This addition brought more size, speed, and style and paved the way for the breed's use in a wider variety of horse sports. The Appaloosa and Paint studbooks were opened to include Quarter Horse and Thoroughbred outcrosses for the same general reasons. American Saddlebred blood was introduced into the Morgan horse breed as a way to increase the show qualities of the breed; some say this has been at the cost of a decline in the breed's historic versatility.

Another example of the homogenization of breeds can be drawn from the development of the European warmblood breeds which now dominate the sports of dressage, driving, eventing, and show jumping around the world. (This group includes the Dutch Warmblood, Hanoverian, Holsteiner, Oldenburg, Selle Francias, Swedish Warmblood, Trakehner, and others.) After World War II, the historic cavalry, driving, and utility breeds were improved through the introduction of Thoroughbred and rigorous selection for athletic performance. The heavy elegance required of carriage horses gave way to lighter, faster horses more suitable for riding sports. Warmblood breed studbooks are kept open to allow for the registration of outstanding individuals from other approved breeds (including Thoroughbred mares) based on excellence in conformation, movement, and performance.

A true breed requires genetic parameters. When assembled based on phenotype and performance, a breed will not be genetically consistent; that is, it will not "breed true." Stringent regulations do not substitute for genetic identity. In contrast to other warmblood breeds, the Cleveland Bay has had a closed studbook in England for over a hundred years. Purebred offspring are of predictable, consistent type, and even partbreds reflect the Cleveland's prepotency. This genetic distinctiveness from the Thoroughbred and other breeds makes the Cleveland Bay a globally significant conservation priority.

A distinct and important class of North American riding horses are the "gaited" breeds, which have gaits in addition to, or instead of the usual walk, trot, and canter. These gaits — which include the fox trot, rack, running walk, single foot, and slow gait — are generally four-beat (rather than the two beats of the trot) making them more comfortable for the rider. Gaited breeds have resulted from long years of selective breeding and divergence from the Thoroughbred type. The American Saddlebred and the Tennessee Walking Horse are the most common of these breeds in North America. The Rocky Mountain Horse (actually developed in the Appalachians) is a rare breed unique to the United States and somewhat distinct from these two popular breeds.

Horse Breed Conservation

The few horse breeds that remain untouched by Thoroughbred and Arabian influence carry traits not present in the major breed groups. As a result, these breeds are the primary reservoir for genetic diversity in the equine species. The diversity they represent is essential for the development of new breeds and uses for horses in the future.

The sixteen horse breeds considered conservation priorities are rare in North America and globally. They can be placed into four groups according to derivation and/or use. There are four draft horse breeds, the American Cream, Clydesdale, Shire, and Suffolk Punch. The Canadian, Cleveland Bay, Friesian, and Hackney were developed as utility breeds for both driving and riding. There are four breeds of specialized riding horses, the Akhal-Teke (from Turkmenistan), Rocky Mountain (from eastern Kentucky), Lipizzan (from Austria), and Spanish Mustang/Spanish Barb, which evolved in the New World from Spanish stocks. Finally, there are four breeds which derive from northern European stocks, the Exmoor and Dartmoor of England, the Gotland of Sweden, and the Sable Island, a feral horse found on Sable Island, Nova Scotia.

Some of these conservation priority breeds are precariously rare, while others are now increasing in popularity. It is of great significance that each one has an association working for its conservation. These breeds depend on the ability of their advocates to promote them for modern uses in sport and recreation without giving into the temptation to crossbreed as a way to conform to a more standardized appearance. It is also imperative that livestock conservation organizations not overlook horses. Conservationists need to work together with breed associations and breeders to provide for long term conservation of the threatened genetic diversity within this species.

Table 10.1
Horse Registrations

In the chart below, data are presented on the number of 1990 purebred registrations, the number of cumulative registrations during the history of the breed, and estimated global populations. These figures better illustrate the status of horse breeds than do 1985 and 1970 registration figures, which primarily reflect changes in the entire industry rather than those of individual breeds. The dates the associations were founded appear in the breed association list.

Breed	Number of Registrations 1990	Cumulative	Estimated Global Population	Data Source[1]
Akhal-Teke	38	73	1,500	s, t
Albino	40	3,259	2,000	s
American Cream Draft	4	248	100	s
American Saddlebred	2,680	215,601	30,000	p, s
Canada	87	3,968	30,000	p
Andalusian	200[a]	1,682	25,000	p, t
Appaloosa	10,669	500,000	300,000	s
Arabian	22,400[a]	450,000	1,000,000	p, s
Canada	1,324	27,892	1,000,000	p
Bashkir Curly	255	1,175	2,000	s
Belgian Draft	3,445	126,070	24,000	p, s
Canada	904	27,367	24,000	p
Buckskin	1,100[a]	22,000[a]	20,000	p
Canadian – Canada	128	5,500	1,000	p, t
Cleveland Bay	(UK) 36[b]		500	s, t
Clydesdale Draft	438	32,000	5,000	s, t
Canada	253	100,108	5,000	p
Colorado Ranger	275	4,166	45,000	p, s
Connemara Pony	59	3,000	15,000	s, t
Dartmoor Pony	8	274	5,000	s
Dutch Warmblood	500	2,000	25,000	p, t
Exmoor Pony	(UK) 105[b]		800	p, s
Friesian	60		6,000	t
Gotland	34	433	8,000	s, t
Hackney Horse/Pony	809	31,352	8,000	s, t
Canada	92	8,505	8,000	p
Haflinger	700	2,400[a]	25,000	p, s, t
Canada	64	279	25,000	p
Hanoverian	300	3,700[a]	30,000	p
Holsteiner	165	1,269	20,000	p, t
Icelandic	187	387	50,000	p, t
Canada	57	476	50,000	p
Lipizzan	83	584	3,000	p, t
Miniature	7,000[a]	50,000[a]	50,000	p, t

Table 10.1 (continued)

Breed	Number of Registrations 1990	Cumulative	Estimated Global Population	Data Source[1]
Missouri Fox Trotter	1,982	35,000	15,000	s, t
Morgan	3,600	118,600	89,000	s
Canada	479	7,369	89,000	p
New Forest Pony	13	165[a]	15,000	p, s
Norwegian Fjord	150[a]	1,000[a]	30,000	p, t
Paint	17,968	193,372	75,000	s
Palomino	2,000[a]	70,000[a]	15,000	p, t
Canada	5	1,934	15,000	p
Paso Fino	1,451	17,059	12,000	t
Percheron Draft	1,200	266,000	20,000	s, t
Canada	667	53,268	20,000	p
Peruvian Paso	1,027	7,484	14,000	s, t
Canada	54	422	14,000	p
Pinto	2,900[a]	66,070	25,000	s
Pony of the Americas	755	37,927	15,000	s
Quarter Horse	110,597	2,900,000	1,800,000	p, s
Canada	61	6,408	1,800,000	p
Rocky Mountain	900	1,700	1,500	s, t
Sable Island – Canada			300	p
Selle Francais	100		20,000	t
Shetland Pony	700	140,000	250,000	p, t
Shire Draft	250[a]		7,000	p, s ,t
Spanish Mustang/Barb	468[a]	5,000	2,500	p, s, t
Standardbred	16,556	683,247	175,000	t
Suffolk Punch	50	3,474	800	s, t
Swedish Warmblood	175[a]		25,000	t
Tarpan	1		150	s, t
Tennessee Walker	7,800	275,000	45,000	s
Canada	84	821	45,000	p
Thoroughbred US and Canada	44,000	1,300,000	2,000,000	p, t
Trekehner	575[a]	7,000[a]	25,000	t
Canada	66	287	25,000	p
Welsh Pony and Cob[c]	597	3,376	200,000	s, t
Canada	190	6,622	200,000	p
Wild Mustang		1,040	20,000	p, s

[1] p = published information; s = survey; t = telephone interview.
[a] Estimate
[b] No registrations were recorded in North America. These British figures approximate global totals.
[c] Figures combine information for Welsh Mountain ponies, Welsh ponies, Welsh ponies of cob type, and Welsh Cobs. There may be fewer than 5,000 Welsh Cobs globally.

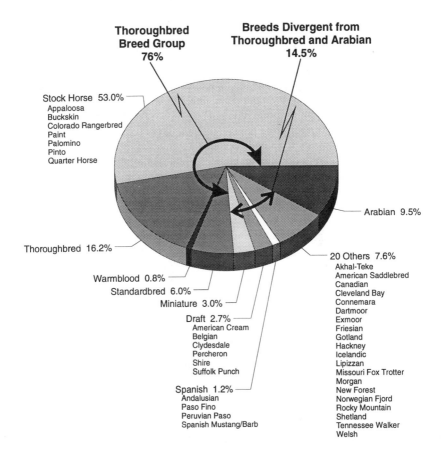

Figure 10.2. North American horse breeds —
1990 registrations by genetic breed group.

Conservation Priority Horse Breeds

Critical: Fewer than 200 annual registrations in North America and an estimated global population of less than 2,000.

Akhal-Teke
American Cream *
Canadian *
Cleveland Bay
Exmoor
Rocky Mountain *
Sable Island (F) *
Suffolk Punch

Rare: Fewer than 1,000 annual registrations in North America and an estimated global population of less than 5,000.

Clydesdale
Dartmoor
Lipizzan
Spanish Mustang/Spanish Barb *

Watch: Fewer than 2,500 annual registrations in North America and an estimated global population of less than 10,000.

Friesian
Gotland
Hackney
Shire

* = Unique to North America
(F) = Feral population or breed of feral origin

A few rare breeds are not included as conservation priorities. The Albino and the Bashkir Curly have open studbooks and so lack necessary genetic parameters. The modern Tarpan is a recreation of the now-extinct wild Tarpan and does not represent a population genetically distinct from its founding stocks.

Horse Breed Associations

(The date in parenthesis is the year the association was founded.)

Akhal-Teke Registry of America (1982), RR 5 Box 110, Staunton, VA 24401; Philip Case, 703-886-1870.

International American **Albino** Association (1937), c/o Summertime Farm, RR 1 Box 20, Naper, NE 68755; 402-832-5560.

American Cream Draft Horse Association (1944), RR 1 Box 30, Charles City, IA 50616; Elizabeth Ziebell.

American Indian Horse Registry (1961), RR 3 Box 64, Lockhart, TX 78644; 512-398-6642.

American Saddlebred Horse Association (1891), 4093 Iron Works Rd, Lexington, KY 40511-8401; 606-259-2742.

American Saddlebred Association of Canada (1948), 220 Melrose Ave, Kitchner, ON N2H 2C1 Canada; 519-745-2827.

International **Andalusian** Horse Association (1979), 1201 S Main St, #D-7, Boerne, TX 78006; 512-249-4027.

Appaloosa Horse Club (1938), PO Box 8403, Moscow, ID 83843; 208-882-5578.

Arabian Horse Registry of America (1908), 12000 Zuni St, Westminster, CO 80234; 303-450-4748.

Canadian **Arabian** Horse Registry (1958), 4445 Calgary Trail South, #300 Terrace Plaza, Edmonton, AB T6H 5R7 Canada; 403-436-4244.

Al Khamsa, Inc. (**Bedouin Arabian**) (1975), 2136 Bethel-Maple Rd, Hammersville, OH 45130; 513-734-1122.

American **Bashkir Curly** Registry (1971), PO Box 453, Ely, NV 89301; 702-289-4228.

Curly Horse Foundation (1990), Box 520, Sunman, IN 47041

Belgian Draft Horse Corporation of America (1887), PO Box 335, Wabash, IN 46992; 219-563-3205.

Canadian **Belgian** Horse Association (1907), c/o Barbara Meyers, RR 3, Schomberg, ON L0G 1T0 Canada; 416-939-7497.

American **Buckskin** Registry Association (1962), PO Box 3850, Redding, CA 96049-3850; 916-223-1420.

International **Buckskin** Horse Association (1971), PO Box 268, Shelby, IN 46377-0268; 219-552-1013.

Sociétié des Eleveurs de Chevaux **Canadiens** (1895), 68 Deslauriers, Pierrefonds, PQ H8Y 2E4 Canada; also, the Upper Canada District of the **Canadian** Horse Breeders Association, c/o Alex Hayward, RR 2, North Gore, ON K0A 2T0 Canada.

Cleveland Bay Horse Society of North America (1886), PO Box 221, South Windham, CT 06266; Martha McCormick, 203-456-8881.

Clydesdale Breeders of the United States (1877), 17378 Kelly Rd, Pecatonica, IL 61063; 815-247-8780.

Clydesdale Horse Association of Canada (1886), c/o Albert Hewsom, RR 2, Thornton, ON L0L 2N0 Canada; 705-458-9214.

Colorado Ranger Horse Association (1938), RR 1 Box 1290, Wampum, PA 16157; 412-535-4841.

American **Connemara** Pony Society (1956), 2630 Hunting Ridge Rd, Winchester, VA 22601; 703-722-2277.

American **Dartmoor** Pony Association (1993), 15870 Pasco-Montra Rd, Anna, OH 45302; 513-596-6623.

Dutch Warmblood/Koninklijk Warmbloed (1983), PO Box 828, Winchester, OR 97495; 503-672-8145.

American **Exmoor** Pony Registry (1987), c/o American Livestock Breeds Conservancy, PO Box 477, Pittsboro, NC 27312; 919-542-5704.

Florida Cracker Horse Association, Inc (1990), PO Box 186, Newberry, FL 32669; Sam Getzen, 904-472-2228.

Friesian Horse Association of North America (1978), 4127 Kentridge Dr SE, Grand Rapids, MI 49508-7913; 616-455-7913.

Galiceno Horse Breeders Association, PO Box 219, Godley, TX 76044.

Swedish **Gotland** Breeders Society (1990), RR 3 Box 134, Corinth, KY 41010; 606-234-5707.

American **Hackney** Horse Society (1891), 4059 Iron Works Rd, Building A, Lexington, KY 40511; 606-255-8694.

Canadian **Hackney** Society (1892), c/o Dr F N Lester, RR 1, Lindsay, ON K9V 4R1 Canada; 705-324-5277.

Haflinger Association of America (1976), 14570 Gratiot Rd, Hemlock, MI 48626; 517-642-5307.

Haflinger Registry of North America (1983), 14640 State Route 83, Coshocton, OH 43812; 614-829-2790.

Canadian **Haflinger** Society (1982), 2 Wadsworth Dr, Ingersoll, ON N5C 2C1 Canada; 519-485-0565.

American **Hanoverian** Society, Inc. (1977), Kentucky Horse Park, 4089 Iron Works Rd, Lexington, KY 40511; 606-255-4141.

Purebred **Hanoverian** Association of American Breeders and Owners, Inc. (1983), PO Box 429, Rocky Hill, NJ 08553; 609-466-9543.

American **Holsteiner** Horse Association (1977), 222 E Main St #1, Georgetown, KY 40324; 502-863-4239.

United States **Icelandic** Federation (1989), 38 Park St, Montclair, NJ 07042; 201-783-3429.

Canadian **Icelandic** Horse Federation, c/o Christine Schwartz, Site 200, Comp 9, RR 1, Vernon, BC V1T 6L4 Canada; 604-545-2336.

Irish Draught Horse Society of North America (1993), 701 Tower Park Rd, RR 1, Sidney, BC V8L 5L7 Canada; 604-656-6899.

United States **Lipizzan** Registry (1980), RR 4 Box 89Y, Amelia, VA 23002; Cheryl Wright, 804-561-2826.

Lipizzan Association of North America, PO Box 1388, Flagstaff, AZ 86001; 602-779-3674.

American **Miniature Horse**, Inc. (1979), 2908 SE Loop 820, Fort Worth, TX 76140; 817-293-0041.

American **Miniature Horse** Registry (1971), PO Box 3415, Peoria, IL 61614; 309-691-9661.

Missouri Fox Trotting Horse Breed Association (1948), PO Box 1027, Ava, MO 65608-1027; 417-683-2468.

American **Morgan** Horse Association (1881), PO Box 960, Shelburne, VT 05482; 802-985-4944.

Canadian **Morgan** Association (1968), Box 3480, Lecuc, AB T9E 6M2 Canada; 403-986-1969.

New Forest Pony Association (1990), PO Box 638, Harrisville, RI 02830; 401-568-8238.

Norwegian Fjord Horse Association of North America (1977), 24570 W Chardon Rd, Grayslake, IL 60030; 708-546-7881.

Norwegian Fjord Horse Registry (1981), PO Box 255, Acworth, NH 03601; 603-835-6932.

Canadian **Fjord** Association (1980), Box 146, Beiseker, AB T0M 0G0, Canada; 403-947-2017.

Oldenburg Association, c/o the International Sporthorse Registry, PO Box 957045, Hoffman Estates, IL 60195; 708-695-8152.

American **Paint** Horse Association (1962), PO Box 961023, Fort Worth, TX 76161; 817-439-3400.

Palomino Horse Association (1936), PO Box 324, Jefferson City, MO 65102; 314-635-5511.

Palomino Horse Breeders of America (1941), 15253 E Skelly Dr, Tulsa, OK 74116-2620; 918-438-1234.

Canadian **Palomino** Horse Association (1952), c/o Laurie Snofl, RR 2, Petersburg, ON N0B 2H0 Canada.

Paso Fino Horse Association (1972), PO Box 600, Bowling Green, FL 33834; 813-375-4331.

Percheron Horse Association of America (1876), PO Box 141, Fredricktown, OH 43019; 614-694-3602.

Canadian **Percheron** Association (1907), c/o Mrs. Cathie James, PO Box 200, Crossfield, AB T0M 0S0 Canada; 403-946-5245.

Peruvian Paso Horse Registry of North America (1970), 1038 4th St #4, Santa Rosa, CA 95404; 707-579-4394.

Peruvian Horse Association of Canada (1985), c/o Shirley McCollister, Lyalta, AB T0J 1Y0 Canada; 403-935-4435.

National **Pinto** Horse Registry (1984), PO Box 486, Oxford, NY 13830; 607-334-4964.

Pinto Horse Association of America (1956), 1900 Samuels Ave, Fort Worth, TX 76102-1141; 817-336-7842.

Pony of the Americas Club (1954), 5240 Elmwood Ave, Indianapolis, IN 46203; 317-788-0107.

American **Quarter Horse** Association (1940), PO Box 200, Amarillo, TX 79168; 806-376-4811.

Canadian **Quarter Horse** Association (1956), 360-800 6th Ave SW, Calgary, AB T2P 3G3 Canada; 403-261-3925.

Rocky Mountain Horse Association (1986), 1140 McCalls Mill Rd, Lexington, KY 40515; 606-263-4374.

Sable Island Horse Committee, c/o Zoe Lucas, PO Box 3504 South, Halifax, NS B3J 3J2 Canada.

North American **Selle Francais** Horse Association (1990), PO Box 646, Winchester, VA 22601; 703-662-2870.

North American **Shagya (Arabian)** Society (1986), RR 2 Box 69, Rochester, MN 55902.

American **Shetland** Pony Club (1888), PO Box 3415, Peoria, IL 61614-3415; 309-691-9661.

American **Shire** Horse Association (1885), 2354 315th Ct, Adel, IA 50003-8011; 515-993-3113.

North American Registry for **English Shires** (1990), 16813 Marengo Rd, Union, IL 60180; 815-923-2040.

Spanish Barb Breeders Association (1972), 188 Springridge Rd, Terry, MS 39170; 601-372-8801.

Southwest **Spanish Mustang** Association (1972), PO Box 48, Finley, OK 74543.

Spanish Mustang Registry (1957), RR 3 Box 7670, Willcox, AZ 85643; 602-384-2886.

U.S. Trotting Association **(Standardbred)** (1932), 750 Michigan Ave, Columbus, OH 43214-1191; 614-224-2291.

American **Suffolk Punch** Association (1910), RR 1 Box 212, Ledbetter, TX 78946; 409-249-5795.

Swedish Warmblood Association, PO Box 1587, Coupeville, WA 98239; 206-678-3503.

American **Tarpan** Record Association (1971), PO Box 1714, Loganville; GA 30249-1714.

Tennessee Walking Horse Breeders and Exhibitors Association (1935), PO Box 286, Lewisburg, TN 37091; 615-359-1574.

Canadian **Walking Horse** Registry (1982), Box 56, Site 2, RR 8, Calgary, AB T2J 2T9 Canada; 403-931-3160.

The Jockey Club **(Thoroughbred)** (1894), 821 Corporate Dr, Lexington, KY 40503; 1-800-444-8521.

Canadian **Thoroughbred** Horse Society, PO Box 172, Rexdale, ON M9W 5L1, Canada; 416-675-1370.

American **Trakehner** Association (1974), 1520 W Church St, Newark, OH 43055; 614-344-1111.

North American **Trakehner** Association (1977), 1660 Collier Rd, Akron, OH 44320; 216-836-9545.

Canadian **Trekehner** Horse Society (1974), Box 1270, New Hamburg, ON N0B 2G0, Canada; 519-662-3209.

Welsh Pony & Cob Society of America (1906), PO Box 2977, Winchester, VA 22601; 703-667-6195.

Welsh Pony & Cob Society of Canada (1979), Box 254, Beeton, ON, L0G 1A0 Canada; 416-729-2806.

Wild Horses of America Registry (1975), 6212 E Sweetwater Ave, Scottsdale, AZ 85254; Karen A. Sussman, 602-991-0273.

Other Resources

American Horse Council, 1700 K Street NW, Suite 300, Washington, DC 20006-3805; 202-296-4031.

The AHC is the trade organization for the entire United States horse industry and publishes an annual *Horse Industry Directory* with a complete list of horse agencies, organizations, publications, and registries, available for $15 from the AHC. *The Economic Impact of the US Horse Industry* (1987) was published by the American Horse Council; the Executive Summary is available from the AHC for $75.

Canadian Horse Council, c/o Les Butler, 155 Queen Street, Suite 1100, Ottawa, ON K1P 6L1, Canada; 613-233-6262.

The *Directory of the Canadian Horse Industry and Buyers Guide* is available at $10.65 each from the Corinthian Publishing Company Ltd, PO Box 670, Aurora, ON L4G 4J9 Canada; 416-727-0107.

---

[1] American Horse Council, *The Economic Impact of the U.S. Horse Industry,* American Horse Council (Washington, DC, 1987).
[2] Karen Kopp Du Teil, "The Elusive Recovery," *Equus* 181, November 1992.
[3] Ibid.

Chapter 11

Sheep

Sheep are ruminants of the genus *Ovis* and, like goats, several species have been domesticated. Sheep have been an important part of North American agriculture since the sixteenth century. In spite of this long history, sheep have always been overshadowed by cattle. A cultural antipathy toward sheep has been fostered by stories of Old West range wars between cattlemen and sheepmen. In more recent history, a generation of GIs came home from World War II with a great disdain for any form of lamb or mutton after a long period of military

Figure 11.1. Navajo Churro sheep.

fare. The cyclical wool market, the incursions of synthetic fibers, the abandonment of our textile industry to other countries, and the traditionally low demand for lamb and mutton have been disincentives for growth in the North American sheep industry. These same factors, along with the relatively low value of individual animals, have also inhibited breed importation from attaining the higher levels seen for cattle and horses.

The sheep industry, however, does have room for expansion. More than 10 percent of the lamb, virtually all sheep dairy products, and a large percentage of wool used in the United States are imported. Many types of sheep production systems are found across North America, from small farm flocks of a dozen or so animals to western range flocks numbering in the thousands.

The existence of management systems from extensive to intensive, diverse climates, and market demands for meat, wool, and dairy products should provide increasing opportunity for the utilization of many differing breeds of sheep. A further demonstration of opportunities available for sheep production is the new American Sheep Industry Association (ASI) *Directory of U.S. Sheep Breeds* which describes 45 breeds of sheep. Still, purebred use lags far behind opportunity. Over one third of the breeds in the ASI brochure are endangered to some degree and are in need of conservation.

Most sheep production systems place very limited emphasis on selection for unique traits or matching of traits to the needs of a specific production plan, but instead are characterized by increasing selection toward uniformity within and between breeds. The show ring has emphasized narrow selection based on large frame, fecundity, rapid gain, and the ability to utilize high grain rations. The result of this narrow selection is that it is now very difficult to distinguish some sheep breeds from one another.

In North America, sheep have been selected primarily for meat. An unpredictable wool market, the labor associated with wool production, vast available rangeland, and inexpensive grain for finishing have all contributed to the selection for meat production. The black faced Suffolk, which accounts for about 36 percent of all registered sheep, enjoys a large part of the lamb market because of its large size and ability to convert concentrates to rapid gain. The most popular white faced breed is the Dorset which comprises about 10 percent of purebred sheep. The Horned Dorset makes up about 10 percent of Dorset registrations, having almost disappeared in the switch to the Polled Dorset. The traditional Horned variety has obvious genetic differences from the Polled, and its conservation is necessary to protect the genetic range of the breed.

Sheep in Agriculture

Sheep are the most multipurpose of our livestock species. They have an important role in sustainable agriculture, not only for the commodities they produce but for the services they render. Of particular value is their role in grassland improvement and integrated pest management. Sheep are being used to control leafy spurge, a vigorous and invasive exotic plant which has been a problem in the West. The United States Forest Service, for example, is using sheep to control brush and weed growth in the Snake River watershed and in the Mount St. Helens volcano recovery area in Washington. Sheep can provide economical and effective vegetation control, particularly where the use of herbicides is a concern, or the terrain too rough for mechanical brush control. Sheep are being used in Vermont to control summer vegetation growth on ski runs; this added service value may encourage the recovery of an historic Vermont sheep industry which has declined in recent years.

"Wherever sheep feet touch the ground, it turns to gold" is an old European adage. Despite the modern stereotype that sheep ruin grassland, under good management sheep can enhance plant diversity and improve the quality of grassland. Their small size means less soil compaction and erosion than with heavier animals. Rotational grazing and mixed grazing with other species actually increases the total forage output from pastures. As ruminants, sheep convert forage which has little nutrient value for humans into high quality food or fiber and so present no competition with humans for food. Grass-fed lamb is also lower in fat and more easily produced for the organic and health food market since "chemical free" grass is easier to procure than equivalent grains and processed feeds.

Agroforestry is recognizing the value of integrating sheep with tree crops. Christmas tree farms offer opportunities for sheep production. These farms have historically been heavy users of pesticides, since the usual restrictions for food crops do not apply. This can lead to problems of pesticide runoff and pollution of surface and ground water. Sheep provide organic pest control and can be a profitable addition to Christmas tree production. St. Croix sheep in particular are the basis of vegetation control in organic macadamia nut production in Hawaii. Sheep have also been used to control understory vegetation and other pests in citrus, rubber, and timber plantations. Profits can be realized not only from the savings in unused chemicals, labor, and equipment, but also in the marketing of grass fed lamb and other sheep products.

Sheep for Fiber Production

There is an irony in the wool market — high demand for finished goods but a global depression of wool prices. Historic fluctuations in the demand for wool have encouraged American sheep producers to select for meat quality and abandon the wool market to other countries. Now, after a long period of decline, many of the wool breeds, such as Jacob, Shetland, and Romney are again gaining recognition for their unique colors and textures.

Of particular interest is the Navajo Churro, which descends from the sheep brought by sixteenth century Spanish explorers and missionaries to their New World missions and outposts. The Navajo Churro breed developed from these stocks, shaped largely by the natural selection of the extreme climate of the desert Southwest. It has a double coat, consisting of a coarse hairy outer layer to deflect the rain and snow and to keep windblown dust and sand from penetrating the fine, insulating undercoat.

Navajo Churro sheep were the basis for a fundamental cultural revolution among the Native American hunter gatherers who became shepherds and weavers. Creativity and spiritualism were expressed in the weavings, which now command international attention in the art world. Mismanagement by the Bureau of Indian Affairs led to the near extinction of this breed in the twentieth century, but the dedicated efforts of Dr. Lyle McNeal, founder of the Navajo Sheep Project of Utah State University, and a handful of other breeders have led to a revival of the breed and the formation of a breed association. As a result, Navajo Churro sheep are being restored to the tribal flocks and now once again provide the raw materials for distinctive tapestries.

Another unusual fiber breed is the Karakul, native to the Middle East but imported to North America a century ago. The breed was historically raised for pelts known as astrakhan or Persian lamb. Astrakhan has been part of the traditional costume over a large area of central Asia for centuries and from time to time it has been a fashion fur in other cultures. North American Karakuls, however, are now being selected to produce spinning fleece as another way to take advantage of the beautiful range of colors and the unusual texture of the fiber. This selection adds to the genetic significance of the North American Karakul population, which has been isolated for so long that it is genetically distinct from Karakuls in the rest of the world.

The growth of specialty wool markets have also led to a renaissance of interest in the longwool breeds: Border Leicester, Cotswold, Lincoln, and Leicester Longwool. Fiber artisans have been rediscovering and promoting these breeds for the texture, color, and lustrous sheen of the fibers. While the Lincoln and Border Leicester are found in reasonably stable populations around the world, the Cotswold has been snatched from the brink of extinction. The Leicester Longwool became extinct in North America and is threatened globally; a new foundation flock was imported in 1989 from Tasmania by Colonial Williamsburg Foundation in Virginia. These animals will be used as the most authentic contemporary breed to interpret eighteenth century agricultural history at Colonial Williamsburg. The imports have done well and several satellite flocks have been established.

Along with the recent rediscovery of the qualities of natural fibers, there is increasing attention paid to the use of sheepskins for clothing, floor coverings, and accessories. Domestic production of sheepskins, however, is handicapped by the limited number of sheepskin tanning facilities; there are now only three in operation in the United States.

Sheep for Dairy Products

Many classic cheeses, including feta, romano, and roquefort, are derived from sheep's milk. Most European countries claim one or more sheep breeds which have been selected for milk production over the course of many centuries. Selection of sheep for dairy characteristics is just beginning in North America, spurred by a growing interest in this potentially lucrative industry. Promising individuals of many traditional breeds such as Tunis, Cotswold, Shropshire, and Dorset are being selected for use in establishing dairy production.

Agriculture Canada has developed two dairy strains based on genetics from the East Friesian sheep, known for its dairy attributes. The Arcott Rideau, and to a lesser extent the Arcott Outouais, are showing significant dairy ability and are in production studies in Canada and at the University of Minnesota.

Within the past ten years several organizations have been formed to support producers and guide the domestic industry. The high level of solids in sheep milk make it particularly valuable for the production of cheese, yogurt, and fudge. A significant advantage to sheep dairying is that sheep's milk freezes and thaws without damage to the manufacturing qualities. It can therefore be stockpiled, frozen, and shipped, allowing seasonal production at any distance from processing plants.

Hair Sheep

Another group of sheep breeds beginning to attract attention is the hair sheep, which do not grow fleece and so do not need to be shorn. Long regarded as useless by American sheep breeders, these animals have unusual attributes which are now being recognized as valuable.

The Barbados Blackbelly, St. Croix, and Puerto Rican Boricua are Caribbean breeds which originated from West African stock. Tropical adaptation has made them heat tolerant, fertile year around, forage efficient, resistant to internal gut parasites, and leaner than temperate climate sheep. The Wiltshire Horn is a large framed British breed which has been documented in North America for over 200 years. This breed was developed for use as a terminal sire for the production of market lambs, but is now globally endangered. The Katahdin is a modern breed developed from a mixture of Wiltshire Horn, Caribbean hair sheep, and some wool breeds. Proponents say that it combines the qualities of large frame and hardiness in a breed which can be used in a variety of climates.

North American Sheep as Genetic Resources

Some globally endangered sheep breeds, including the Cotswold and the Lincoln, have significant North American populations. Other breeds, such as the Gulf Coast Native and the Navajo Churro, are unique to this continent. The Tunis and Karakul represent American populations long divergent from other broad tailed sheep around the world and should now be considered American breeds. The Tunis, for example, came originally from North Africa over two centuries ago and has become quite different from its foundation stock.

North America also has genetically unique populations of feral sheep, that is, free ranging populations which have descended from escaped domestic stocks. The Santa Cruz Island and Hog Island sheep were both populations long-isolated on islands where unique environmental pressures have been very different than those selection pressures associated with production management. These animals have gained a hardiness generated by natural selection and have evolved through genetic drift or genetic segregation to exhibit unique genetic traits. While these breeds may not have an obvious role in today's commercial sheep production, prudence dictates a careful look at the genetic attributes before the feral populations are discarded.

Stringent health restrictions now inhibit the movement of sheep between countries. The low economic value of individual animals is also unlikely to support the cost of documentation, health testing, and quarantine which is necessary for importation into North America. Technologies for artificial insemination and embryo transfer are not as well developed for sheep as for cattle. All of these factors increase the isolation of the North American genetic pool and increase both the genetic value and the threat of extinction to breeds with low population numbers.

Trends

The future looks bright for small ruminants, especially sheep, in North America. Sheep are well adapted to grazing on land not otherwise suited for crops. The services of sheep in control of invasive plant growth on range land, sensitive watersheds, and in agroforestry are attractive. The environmental impact of sheep is relatively low, and minimal management is necessary for the production of lean meat. While the value of wool is not currently high, the market for natural fibers remains strong and the wool industry could benefit by advances in processing and marketing. Sheep dairy products are a high value commodity which have yet to be fully developed in this country.

Since small ruminants are likely to play an increasingly important role in providing high quality food for the developed as well as the developing world, North American sheep genetic resources are well worth safeguarding.

Table11.1
Sheep Registrations

The data on sheep registrations for 1990, 1985, and 1970 are listed alphabetically by breed, with the figures for the United States followed by Canadian registration figures. In some breeds (Arcott, Icelandic, Leicester Longwool, and Romanov) all North American animals are registered with the Canadian Livestock Record Corporation.

Breed	Number of Registrations			Date Association Founded	Data Source[1]
	1990	1985	1970		
Arcott – Canada					
Canadian	110				p, t
Outaouais	118				p, t
Rideau	282				p, t
Barbados	Information not available				
Black Welsh Mountain	205	100		1991	p, s
Blueface Leicester	50[a]				s, t
Border Leicester	411				p, t
Canada	426	421			p
Cheviot	2,800	2,537	2,807	1891	p
Canada	78	111			p
Clun Forest	155	161		1973	s, t
Canada	77	38			p
Columbia	9,512	8,007	6,442	1942	p
Canada	224	203			p
Cormo	50			1975	p
Coopworth	1,800			1986	p, t
Corriedale	5,050	4,453	9,050	1916	p
Canada	122	129			p
Cotswold	178	116	23	1878	p, s, t
Canada	22	16			p
Delaine Merino	648	856	1,300	1885	p, s
Dorset (Polled/Horn)	16,878	12,800	9,336	1898	p, t
Dorset Horn	1,498				t
Canada (Polled/Horn)	2,422	1,772			p
Finnsheep	930	890		1971	p, s
Gulf Coast Native	150[a]			1985	t
Hampshire	17,407	16,475	21,360	1889	p
Canada	684	674			p
Hog Island	20[a]	10[a]			t
Icelandic – Canada	70				p
Jacob Sheep	652	100		1988	p, s
Canada	13				p
Karakul	183	148		1929	s, t
Canada	24	1			p
Katahdin	825	100		1986	s, t

Leicester Longwool – Canada	25	2		1888	p, s, t
Lincoln	731	386	245	1889	p
Canada	160	169			p
Montadale	3,404	3,006	3,000	1945	p
Navajo Churro	543	100		1986	s
North Country Cheviot	827	540		1962	p, s
Canada	567	489			p
Oxford	1,890	1,564	2,400	1882	p
Canada	310	211			p
Polypay	11,429			1979	p
Canada	247				p
Rambouillet	16,000	11,026	4,500	1889	p
Canada	685	131			p
Romanov – Canada	1,802				p
Romney	2,600	1,600	1,000	1912	p
Canada	150	59			p
Santa Cruz Island	50[a]				s, t
Scottish Blackface	250	100		1982	t
Shetland	385			1991	s, t
Shropshire	3,418	3,433	5,215	1884	p
Canada	68	94			p
Southdown	5,800	4,839	5,677	1882	p
Canada	354	286			p
St. Croix	300	135		1988	s, t
Suffolk	70,320	67,831	38,920	1929	p, s
Canada	4,246	4,508			p
Targhee	2,935	1,816	650	1951	s
Canada	25	55			p
Texel	No information available			1991	p, t
Tunis	583	410	200	1896	p
Wiltshire Horn	30[a]	10			t

[1] p = published information; s = survey; t = telephone interview.
[a] No registry exists or the registry data are not complete. This is an estimate of the purebreds born in North America.

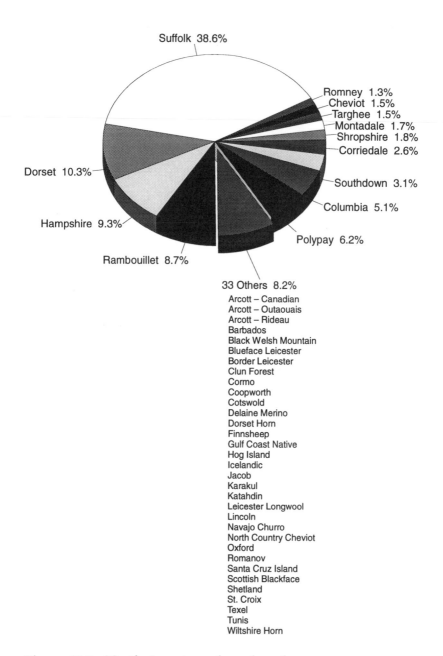

Suffolk 38.6%

Romney 1.3%
Cheviot 1.5%
Targhee 1.5%
Montadale 1.7%
Shropshire 1.8%
Corriedale 2.6%

Dorset 10.3%

Southdown 3.1%

Columbia 5.1%

Hampshire 9.3%

Polypay 6.2%

Rambouillet 8.7%

33 Others 8.2%

Arcott – Canadian
Arcott – Outaouais
Arcott – Rideau
Barbados
Black Welsh Mountain
Blueface Leicester
Border Leicester
Clun Forest
Cormo
Coopworth
Cotswold
Delaine Merino
Dorset Horn
Finnsheep
Gulf Coast Native
Hog Island
Icelandic
Jacob
Karakul
Katahdin
Leicester Longwool
Lincoln
Navajo Churro
North Country Cheviot
Oxford
Romanov
Santa Cruz Island
Scottish Blackface
Shetland
St. Croix
Texel
Tunis
Wiltshire Horn

Figure 11.2. North American sheep breeds —
a comparison of purebred registrations for 1990.

Conservation Priority Sheep Breeds

Critical: Fewer than 200 annual registrations in North America and an estimated global population of less than 2,000.

Cotswold
Gulf Coast Native *
Hog Island (F) *
Leicester Longwool
Santa Cruz (F) *
Wiltshire Horn

Rare: Fewer than 1,000 annual registrations in North America and an estimated global population of less than 5,000.

Clun Forest
Delaine Merino
Karakul
Katahdin *
Lincoln
Navajo Churro *
St. Croix *
Tunis *

Watch: Fewer than 2,500 annual registrations in North America and an estimated global population of less than 10,000.

Black Welsh Mountain
Dorset Horn
Jacob
North Country Cheviot
Oxford
Shetland

Study: Populations of genetic interest which lack breed definition or documentation.

Barbados (Caribbean and mainland) *
Boricua (Puerto Rican hair sheep) *

* = Unique to North America
(F) = Feral population or breed of feral origin

A few breeds are rare in North America but are not considered conservation priorities. These include the following breeds, which are globally numerous: Blueface Leicester, Coopworth, Finnsheep, Icelandic, Romanov, and Scottish Blackface. The Arcott breeds and the Cormo were recently developed from numerically strong foundation stocks and are also not listed as being in need of conservation.

Sheep Breed Associations

Bluefaced Leicester, RR 1 Box 595, Middletown, VA 22645; J. Frank Baylis, 703-869-6286.

American **Border Leicester** Association, RR 4 Box 138, Taylorsville, NC 28681; Kris Savage, 704-632-6529.

North American **Border Leicester** Association, 39282 River Dr, Lebanon, OR 97355; R. J. Harward, 503-258-2373.

American **Cheviot** Sheep Club, RR 1 Box 100, Clarks Hill, IN 47930; Ruth Bowles, 317-523-2193.

North American **Clun Forest** Association, W855 Mahlum Rd, Holmen, WI 54636; E. K. Reedy, 608-526-4101.

Columbia Sheep Breeders Association of America, PO Box 272E, Upper Sandusky, OH 43351; R. L. Gerber, 614-482-2608.

Coopworth Society of North America, 1335 West U Ave, Schoolcraft, MI 49087; Matt Wiley, 616-344-2152.

Cormo Sheep Association, RR 59, Broadus, MT 59317; Charlotte Carlert, 406-427-5449.

American **Corriedale** Association, PO Box 29C, Seneca, IL 61360; Russell E. Jackson, 815-357-6339.

American **Cotswold** Record Association, PO Box 59, 18 Elm St, Plympton, MA 02367; Vicki Rigel, 617-585-2026.

American **Delaine Merino** Record Association, 1026 County Road 1175, Ashland, OH 44805-9523; E. Clouser, 419-281-5786.

Blacktop **Delaine Merino** Breed Association, 1775 Damman Rd, Fowlerville, MI 48836; James Sober, 517-223-9728.

Continental **Dorset** Club, PO Box 506, Hudson, IA 50643; Marion A. Meno, 319-988-4122.

Finnsheep Breeders Association, PO Box 512, Zionsville, IN 46077-0512; Claire Carter, 317-873-3597.

Gulf Coast Native Sheep Registry, c/o American Livestock Breeds Conservancy, PO Box 477, Pittsboro, NC 27312; 919-542-5704.

American **Hampshire** Sheep Association, PO Box 377, Whiteland, IN 46184; Karey Claghorn, 317-535-7601.

Hog Island Sheep Registry, c/o American Livestock Breeds Conservancy, PO Box 477, Pittsboro, NC 27312; 919-542-5704.

Jacob Sheep Breeders Association, 6350 E County Road 56, Fort Collins, CO 80524-9340, Janine Fenton 303-484-3344.

Jacob Sheep Conservancy, 9241 Eureka Rd, Girard, PA 16417; Colleen Kozlowski, 814-474-3503.

American **Karakul** Sheep Registry, 3026 Thomas Rd, Rice, WA 99167; Julie DeVlieg, 509-738-6310.

Katahdin Hair Sheep International, RR 1, Fairview KS 66425; Laura Callan Fortmeyer, 913-467-8041.

Leicester Longwool, c/o Colonial Williamsburg Foundation, PO Box 1776, Williamsburg, VA 23187-1776; Elaine Shirley, 804-229-1000.

National **Lincoln** Sheep Breeders Association, RR 6 Box 24, Decatur, IL 62521; Teresa M. Kruse, 217-864-3601.

Montadale Sheep Breeders Association, PO Box 603, Plainfield, IN 46168; Mildred Brown, 317-839-6198.

Navajo Churro Sheep Association, Taos Junction Box 494, Ojo Caliente, NM 87549; Connie Taylor.

American **North Country Cheviot** Association, PO Box 265, Lula, GA 30554; Theresa Barefoot, 404-869-7726.

American **Oxford** Sheep Association, Rt 1 Box 75, Stonington, IL 62567; Mary Blome, 217-325-3515.

American **Polypay** Sheep Association, 609 S Central #6, Sidney, MT 59270; Linda Wick.

American **Rambouillet** Sheep Breeders Association, 2709 Sherwood Way, San Angelo, TX 76901; Joann Custer, 915-949-4414.

North American **Romanov** Sheep Association, PO Box 1296, Pataskala, OH 43062-1296; Don Kirts, 614-927-3098.

Romanov Sheep Breeders Association of Canada, c/o 313 Cartwright, Providence, MB R0K 0LA, Canada; Floyd Schrams, 204-529-2309.

Romanov Sheep Center, 49800 Township Road 58, Lewisville, OH 43754-9436; David Blackstone, 614-567-3463.

American **Romney** Breeders Association, 29515 NE Weslinn Dr, Corvallis, OR 97333.

St. Croix Sheep Breeders Association, c/o Cole Evans, Department of Animal Science, Utah State University, Logan, UT 84322-4815.

Santa Cruz Island Sheep Registry, c/o American Livestock Breeds Conservancy, PO Box 477, Pittsboro, NC 27312; 919-542-5704.

Scottish Blackface Sheep Breeders Association, 30282 River Dr, Lebanon, OR 97355; R. J. Harward, 503-258-2373.

North American **Shetland** Sheep Registry, 1240 N 22nd St, Allegan, MI 49010; Linda Zuppann, 616-673-5809.

American **Shropshire** Registry, PO Box 250, Hebron, IL 60034; Dale Blackburn, 815-648-4750.

American **Southdown** Breeders Association, HC 13 Box 220, Fredonia, TX 76842; Gary Jennings, 915-429-6226

American **Suffolk** Sheep Society, PO Box 256, Newton, UT 84327; Roger Sanders, 801-563-6105.

National **Suffolk** Sheep Association, PO Box 617, Columbia, MO 65205; Kathy K Krafka, 314-442-4103.

U.S. **Targhee** Sheep Associaton, PO Box 15, Jasper, MN 56144; Debra Mrozinski, 507-348-7905.

North American **Texel** Sheep Association, RR 1 Box 927, Laurel, MS 39440; Linda Gayle Smith, 601-426-2264.

National **Tunis** Sheep Registry, RR 1 Box 192, Gouverneur, NY 13642; Lyle Hotis, 315-287-3776.

Wiltshire Horn Sheep Registry, c/o American Livestock Breeds Conservancy, PO Box 477, Pittsboro, NC 27312; 919-542-5704.

Other Resources

American Sheep Industry Association, 6911 S Yosemite St, Englewood, CO 80112-1414; 303-771-3500.

Canadian Livestock Records Corporation, 2417 Holly Lane, Ottawa, ON K1V 0M7, Canada; 613-731-7110.

Canadian Sheep Breeders Association, Box 260, Borden, SK S0K 0N0 Canada; Rita Widgill, 306-997-4881 (combined breeds association in Canada).

U.S. Sheep and Goat Industry: Council for Agricultural Science and Technology report No. 94, May 1982, and No. 101, September 1984.

U.S. Sheep Industry Market Report, 1990–91.

Chapter 12

Swine

While there are a number of genera and species of wild pig, all domestic breeds originate from the European Wild Boar, *Sus scrofa*. Swine and poultry provide the greatest amount of animal protein world wide, and yet they are now the most genetically endangered livestock species.

Historically, breed improvement in swine has lagged considerably behind that of horses, cattle, and sheep because swine production was almost a sideline of other agricultural enterprises. These adaptable

Figure 12.1. Tamworth swine.

animals were raised with little management and they were able to convert farm and kitchen waste, forage, and wild mast into pork for home use or for a cash crop. Even as market demand increased, swine production did not capture the imagination of creative agriculturalists to the same degree as did the other species. An exception to this generalization was the Berkshire pig, which rose to great social heights in the late 1800s, particularly in England, where the aristocracy included improvement of swine breeds in its enthusiasm for an enlightened agriculture.

In contrast, selection for improvement in swine now proceeds at a breakneck pace. Swine breeds are being selected as uniform, high production animals using maximum nutritional input, sophisticated husbandry, and close confinement. Producers have responded to the loss in value of lard as a commodity by reshaping swine into a new lean form. Rapid growth, with an emphasis on muscle development, gets animals to market early, well before fat deposition results from the high nutrient feeding. As a result of this selection, the number of breeds has decreased dramatically, and the differences among breeds are being lost. This has an important implication, since breed differences are the basis for hybrid vigor, the driving force in commercial production programs.

Pork production is becoming industrialized, not just in North America, but globally. Multinational corporations are establishing confinement swine production facilities in developing countries where labor is cheap. Confinement facilities, wherever they are located, are generally uniform in equipment, management, feed, and genetic stocks. The result of this rush to uniformity is a continuing erosion of genetic diversity parallel to that occurring in the poultry industry.

In the United States, nearly 50 percent of pork processing is controlled by four corporations.[1] Pork production is also becoming more centralized, as the number of hog producers has declined drastically in the last 20 years. In 1974, there were nearly 750,000 hog producers; by 1993, there were only 265,000. At the same time, producers marketing over 50,000 hogs per year increased their volume by 25 percent in 1990–1991 alone. Many of these new mega-producers are already mega-processors. Even the number of packing plants has become centralized, with 30 percent of plants being closed in the last ten years, thus reducing independent producers' access to facilities.[2] The percentage of pork produced under contract continues to grow. For example, in Pennsylvania over 60 percent of pork is now produced by contract growers instead of independent farmers.[3] This means that the selection and control of genetic stocks is being transferred from farmers to multinational corporations.

One bright spot for independent breeding stock producers is a new method of on-farm performance evaluation. The Purebred Swine

Association in the United States has recently developed a computer program for performance testing which may have a positive effect on the production of purebred breeding stock. When swine farmers have access to performance statistics in addition to their skills in visual selection, they will then be able to market animals on the basis of predicted performance. The initial result of this on-farm evaluation program has been a recent increase in the number of purebred swine registrations in the major commercial breeds, though the impact on rarer breeds has yet to be ascertained.

A Recent History of the Swine Industry

Of the 15 distinct swine breeds listed in the USDA *Agriculture Yearbook 1930*, over half have now disappeared. A recent study by the American Livestock Breeds Conservancy indicates that two-thirds of the livestock breeds documented as extinct in North America are swine breeds. This is no doubt due to the incredible market changes of the past 60 years.

"To market, to market to buy a fat pig. Home again, home again, jiggity jig."

Prior to World War II, lard was an important product of the American swine industry. Lard was the major North American cooking fat and an important manufacturing resource. Not only were Americans urged to recycle cooking fats during the war by returning them to the butcher, they were also encouraged to switch to vegetable oils for cooking so that animal fats could be used for munitions manufacture. This substitution of vegetable fat for animal fat continued after the war.

"Jack Spratt would eat no fat."

Fat consumption as a health issue has received increasing attention in the past few decades. This health concern accelerated the decline in the use of lard and other animal fats, with a resulting decline in the economic value of these fats. The response of the industry was to select pigs for rapid weight gains, with special attention to muscle growth rather than fat deposition.

Most of the traditional swine breeds in North America were selected historically to use a variety of forages and feeds and to lay on as much fat as possible. But the market demanded change. In general, those breeds which were most numerous received the most intense selection to fit the new market. For example, Poland China, Berkshire, Yorkshire, and Duroc had all been valuable lard producers but were transformed into meat producers. In the process they became barely recognizable as the breeds that previously existed. Other breeds were ignored by the selection process either because they were too few in number or because they did not fit well into the more intensive production programs. Those breeds which were not changed generally fell into decline.

"Barber, barber, shave a pig, how many hairs to make a wig?"

Wigs made of pig bristles may not seem an especially elegant product, but the 1876 Centennial Exposition Building in Washington, DC, displays a full wall of pig bristle brushes — including hair brushes, paint brushes, shaving brushes, dusting brushes, and others. Pig bristle production was historically an important part of the swine industry. Synthetic bristles are now used for our brushes, and so the pig has lost another job. Since swine are now raised indoors, without the need of hair to keep them warm or pigment to protect them from sunburn, they can be selected to be big, white, and hairless — also the preference of the processor.

Conservation Priority Breeds

The selection for white pigs in the United Kingdom and throughout most of Europe has been so intense that all the colored pig breeds are in grave danger. Among several of the rare British breeds found in small numbers in North America are Gloucester Old Spot, Large Black, and Saddleback. These breeds are kept by a very few people without the support of breed associations and are in imminent danger of global extinction.

One exception to the gloomy trend for British colored swine is the ginger red Tamworth, which is now more plentiful in the United States than in the United Kingdom. Though by no means in the commercial mainstream, this breed is increasing in numbers in North America and gaining attention as a hardy outdoor pig, particularly in the South where its coloration helps protect against sunburn. The boars are known for getting their job done with efficiency in pasture breeding programs.

The modern Berkshire has been successful in the United States, but the breed has nearly disappeared in Canada. The "Berk" (pronounced "bark" in many quarters) is one of the traditional swine breeds which has been modified to meet today's market needs, though the modern breed bears little resemblance to its forebears. A few breeders in the United States and Canada maintain Berkshire lines of the traditional type.

Other uniquely American swine breeds are also threatened. The Hereford swine fills a niche in the northern Great Plains similar to the Tamworth in the South. A strong regional following and an active breed association support this breed. Hereford swine have been selected for the same color pattern as Hereford cattle as well as hardiness for outdoor production.

The original Guinea Hog was a breed type documented as a large, red, African breed reaching America in the 1700s and 1800s as a consequence of the slave trade. The original Guinea Hog type had disappeared by the turn of the century, and its link with later populations of Guinea Hogs is not clear.

The breed name Guinea Hog is now used to describe small, black homestead pigs known throughout the Southeast during the twentieth century. The breed found favor as a homestead pig for the lard and pork it produced while living off acorns, nuts, and roots foraged in the woods. A Guinea Hog was often collared and kept in the yard to control snakes. As fewer people kept homestead hogs, the breed declined dramatically. In effect, it has lost its habitat. The breed has also suffered from lack of organization and definition. A recently formed breeders association should aid in its conservation.

The Mulefoot was a well-established North American breed with several breed associations at the turn of the twentieth century. It was a black pig, often with white points, used for lard as well as for meat. The breed name Mulefoot describes its most prominent trait, a solid hoof, like that of a mule, but this was just one of the characteristics along with color, conformation, and ear set which marked the breed. Today, the Mulefoot is nearly extinct. There are still "mulefooted" swine to be seen, but these animals are more likely the result of the common genetic mutation syndactylism (which may occur in any breed) rather than representatives of the historic breed. Documentation of the various mulefooted populations is a priority to determine if the true Mulefoot still survives.

Ossabaw Island swine are of special conservation interest for two reasons. First, the breed is an historic relict found only in North America, on Ossabaw Island off the coast of Georgia. Ossabaw swine descend directly from those animals brought by Spanish explorers in the 1500s and are the closest living representatives of this historic type. Second, the breed has been shaped by the difficult environment of the island. Natural selection has made it physiologically unique in that it stores large amounts of fat as a way of coping with a very scarce food supply in the spring. This physiology is a form of non-insulin dependent diabetes, making Ossabaw Island swine an excellent research model for the disease as well as for the impact of natural selection on a complex biological process.

The swine population on Ossabaw Island is healthy, but its uncontrolled reproductive success threatens destruction of its habitat. There is also concern that this population has the potential to harbor disease which might threaten the mainland swine industry. Some small breeding groups have been established on the mainland, though these populations immediately lose the selection pressure of the island and, eventually, the unique adaptive genetic traits will be lost. It is therefore important to maintain some animals *in situ* and to continue to document the breed's unique genetic adaptations.

The Future for Swine

Swine have a significant role to play in diversified farming — as land clearers, compost turners, and omnivorous pest and waste recyclers. The traditional use of swine in orchards is, unfortunately, now limited due to high pesticide loads in fruit crops.

The obstacles facing such creative uses of hogs are numerous. Many of the skills of extensive management of hogs have been lost, and research on the most efficient extensive management systems is sorely needed. Breed specific research is of particular importance, as the performance of the swine species in extensive husbandry should not be judged solely by the performance of breeds selected for confinement. The Tamworth and other traditional swine breeds may prove superior, particularly where reproduction and other biological functions are measured in addition to growth rate.

A major concern for extensive and small scale swine operations lies in the decreasing availability of processing facilities, as production shifts from independent farmers to contract growers. Access to processing facilities is essential if farmers are to profit from the high value pork they are able to produce. Without market opportunities for independent swine farmers, endangered breeds cannot be conserved.

Table 12.1
Swine Registrations

Since there are so few swine breeds, this table has been arranged in order of population level to dramatically demonstrate the differences in breed populations.

The major swine breed registries changed from registration of individual animals to registration of litters between the 1985 and 1990 inventories. This change has had the effect of increasing the registration numbers for the major breeds; in the past, not all individuals in every litter were registered. For this report, litter registrations of the major breeds have been adjusted by a factor of ten (pigs per litter) to generate an estimated number of individual registrations, which can be compared to earlier figures.

Breed	Number of Registrations			Date Association Founded	Data Source[1]
	1990	1985	1970		
Gloucester Old Spot	36	50			t
Guinea Hog	50			1991	t
Ossabaw Island	52	(hundreds on Ossabaw Island)			t
Large Black	200[a]				t
Canada	37	0	421		t
Red Wattle	200[a]				t
Canada	72			1984	p, t
Saddleback	200[a]				t
Canada	0	3	52		p
Hereford	400	358	317	1934	p, s
Tamworth	2,490	1,950	1,000	1923	s
Canada	32	39	97		p
Poland China	18,480	23,180	11,191	1876	p
Canada	3	0	90		p
Berkshire	20,710	21,580	7,210	1875	p
Canada	37	14	26		p
Landrace	43,650	35,010	6,123	1950	t
Canada	8,450	7,068		1955	p
Chester White	55,440	51,580	16,456	1930	p
Canada	9	17	112		p
Spotted	64,430	93,100	13,974	1914	t
Canada	39	141	10		p
Hampshire	189,250	141,170	74,101	1893	t
Canada	1,573	1,317	3,554		p
Yorkshire	206,000	217,000	56,500	1935	s
Canada	9,026	9,536	11,735		p
Duroc	221,790	218,520	62,830	1957	p, t
Canada	3,188	1,804	1,027		p
Pot Bellied	Registries will not provide data				s, t

[1] p = published information; s = survey; t = telephone interview.
[a] Estimated numbers of purebred offspring.

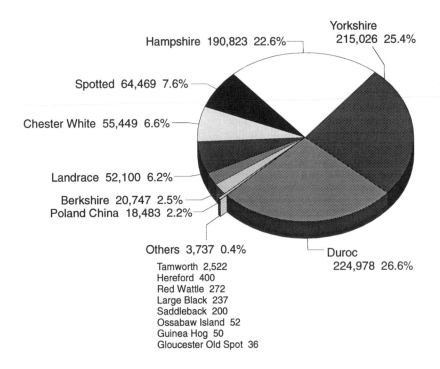

Yorkshire
215,026 25.4%

Hampshire 190,823 22.6%

Spotted 64,469 7.6%

Chester White 55,449 6.6%

Landrace 52,100 6.2%

Berkshire 20,747 2.5%
Poland China 18,483 2.2%

Others 3,737 0.4%

Tamworth 2,522
Hereford 400
Red Wattle 272
Large Black 237
Saddleback 200
Ossabaw Island 52
Guinea Hog 50
Gloucester Old Spot 36

Duroc
224,978 26.6%

Figure 12.2. North American swine breeds —
a comparison of purebred registrations for 1990.

Conservation Priority Swine Breeds

Critical: Fewer than 200 annual registrations in North America and an estimated global population of less than 2,000.

Gloucester Old Spot
Large Black
Ossabaw Island (F) *
Saddleback

Rare: Fewer than 1,000 annual registrations in North America and an estimated global population of less than 5,000.

Hereford *

Watch: Fewer than 2,500 annual registrations in North America and an estimated global population of less than 10,000.

Tamworth

Study: Populations of genetic interest which lack breed definition or documentation.

Guinea Hog *
Mulefoot *
Red Wattle *

* = Unique to North America
F = Feral population or breed of feral origin

The Pot Bellied pig breeds are not considered conservation priorities, since they are not globally endangered. In general, the volatility of the pet pig market has led to increasingly confused breed definition. Other breeds (including the Guinea Hog and the Ossabaw) have been added to the pet population and the multitude of breed names obscures more than it reveals about genetic origins.

Swine Breed Associations

American **Berkshire** Association, Box 2436, West Lafayette, IN 47906; Jack Wall, 317-497-3618.

Chester White Swine Record, 1803 W Detweiller Dr, Peoria, IL 61615; Dan Parrish, 309-692-1571.

United **Duroc** Swine Registry, 1803 W Detweiller Dr, Peoria, IL 61615; Gary Huffington, 309-691-8094.

Canadian **Duroc** Swine Club, c/o Joyce Needham, CP 1007, Bedford, PQ JOJ 10A, Canada.

Gloucester Old Spot, There is currently no association; for information, contact George Bruns, 5142 W Jefferson, Springfield, IL 62707; 217-546-6637.

Guinea Hog Association, 14335 Pauma Vista Dr. Valley Center, CA 92082; Gabriella Nanci, 619-749-2126.

Hampshire Swine Registry, 6748 N Frostwood Parkway, Peoria, IL 61615; Rick Maloney, 309-692-1571.

Canadian **Hampshire** Club, 41 Culpepper St, Waterloo, ON N2L 5KB, Canada; Herb Woodhouse.

National **Hereford** Hog Record Association, RR 1 Box 37, Flandreau, SD 57028; Ruby Schrecengost, 605-997-2116.

American **Landrace** Association, PO Box 2340, W Lafayette, IN 47906; Don Verhoff, 317-497-3718.

Canadian **Landrace** Swine Breeders, PO Box 34, Beebe, PQ JOB 1EO, Canada; Al Smith, 819-876-5103.

Large Black, There is no association; for information, contact Mike Butcher, RR 3 Box 68, Palmyra, IL 62674; 217-484-6482.

American **Miniature Pig** Association, Inc., PO Box 116, Douglasville, GA 30153.

Ossabaw Island, There is no association; for information, contact the American Livestock Breeds Conservancy, PO Box 477, Pittsboro, NC 27312; 919-542-5704.

Poland China Record Association, PO Box 2537, West Lafayette, IN 47906; Todd Boicken, 317-497-3818.

Pot Bellied Pig Registry Service, 20471 Rockstroh Rd, Lakeville, IN 46536; 219-784-8105.

Animal Registry (**Red Wattle**), RR 1 Box 112, Terril, IA 51364; Ruth Preston, 712-853-6372.

Animal Research Foundation (**Red Wattle**), RR 2 Box 1480, Quinlan, TX 75474; 903-356-2267.

Wenglar's **Red (Wattle) Waddle** Hog Association, RR 7 Box 153, Jacksonville, TX 75766; Mrs. Wengler, 903-586-6138.

Saddleback Registry, PO Box 41, Eldridge, AL 35554; Manley and Keith Norris, 205-924-8572.

National **Spotted** Swine Record, 1803 W Detweiller Dr, Peoria, IL 61615; Dan Parrish, 309-693-1804.

Tamworth Swine Association, 200 Centenary Rd, Winchester, OH 45697; Thomas Fenton, Jr., 513-695-0114.

International **Vietnamese/Chinese** Pig Association, PO Box 717, Grass Valley, CA 95945; 916-489-2118.

American **Yorkshire** Club, Inc., PO Box 2417, West Lafayette, IN 47906; Darrell D. Anderson, 317-463-3593.

Canadian **Yorkshire** Club, RR 2, Tavistock, ON N0B 2R0, Canada; Warren Stein.

For information on Canadian breed populations contact:

Canadian Swine Breeders Association, RR 3, Embro, ON N0J 1J0, Canada; Karen Sample, 519-475-4806; and the **Purebred Swine Breeders Association of Canada**, 2417 Holly Lane, Ottawa, ON K1V 7P2 Canada.

Other Resources

ATTRA, Appropriate Technology Transfer for Rural Areas has information available on livestock use in sustainable agriculture. Among several good publications is *Sustainable Swine Production*. For more information, contact ATTRA, PO Box 3657, Fayetteville, AR 72702, 1-800-346-9140.

National Pork Producers Council, PO Box 10383, Des Moines, IA 50306

---

[1] V. J. Rhodes, *Missouri Pork Industry,* 1988; and *Hog Farm Management*, September 1989.
[2] Alexander Rhoads, "Hog Tied: The decline of family farm hog production," *Prairie Journal*, Winter 1992–1993.
[3] *Purebred Picture*, "The Shock Family of Pennsylvania," June 1992.

Chapter 13

Census Summary

$\mathbf{A}$griculture — like any other biological system — is entirely dependent on genetic diversity for future adaptation, selection, and improvement. A great variety of animals and plants from around the world have been the foundation for success in North American agriculture.

Dramatic genetic erosion is now occurring within the livestock species in North America and throughout the world. The livestock industry relies on fewer and fewer breeds to satisfy the needs of producer and consumer, while other breeds are cast aside as unworthy of use. These "unwanted" breeds, however, represent much of the genetic diversity remaining in the livestock species. Their conservation is an insurance policy necessary for agriculture to face the challenges of an unknown future.

The first step of any conservation program is to understand the nature of the problem. The American Livestock Breeds Conservancy has conducted a census of all livestock breeds in the United States and Canada and herein reports these census data and analyzes trends currently affecting livestock breeds and species.

Almost two hundred breeds of asses, cattle, goats, horses, sheep, and swine in North America were examined. The data show that nearly 80 breeds have very low numbers, and some are facing extinction. About half of ass, goat, sheep, and swine breeds, one third of cattle breeds, and nearly one quarter of horse breeds are in need of active conservation efforts.

It is naive to assume that the primary cause of increase or decrease in a breed's numbers is its merit relative to other breeds. In reality, broad trends in agriculture and society which determine how agriculture is practiced have more impact on the array and status of breeds than do breed characteristics. Several trends inherent in modern agriculture have increased genetic erosion: uniform selection of industrial stocks; substitution of human resources, capital, and chemicals for animals' natural abilities; devaluation of purebred livestock; consolidation of agricultural resources; and attitudes favoring standardization in agricultural methods and products.

The North American Livestock Census demonstrates the urgent need to conserve livestock genetic diversity and includes recommendations for breed conservation programs in North America. If these conservation programs succeed, there will be little genetic erosion within the livestock species. If they fail, there will be increased loss of genetic diversity in livestock and consequently greatly restricted opportunity in animal agriculture of the future.

Conservation Categories

Critical: Fewer than 200 annual registrations in North America and an estimated global population of less than 2,000.

Rare: Fewer than 1,000 annual registrations in North America and an estimated global population of less than 5,000.

Watch: Fewer than 2,500 annual registrations in North America and an estimated global population of less than 10,000. (Also included are dairy cattle breeds which show marked decline in numbers over the last 20 years.)

Study: Populations of genetic interest which lack breed definition or documentation.

Table 13.1
A Summary of the American Livestock Breeds Conservancy's North American Livestock Census

Critical	Rare	Watch	Study
Asses			
American Mammoth Jackstock*		Miniature Donkey	
Poitou			

Cattle

Ankole Watusi	Belted Galloway	Ayrshire	
Devon	Canadienne*	British White	
Dutch Belted	Dexter	Guernsey	
Florida Cracker*	Galloway	Highland	
Herens		Milking Shorthorn	
Kerry		Red Poll	
Milking Devon*		Senepol*	
Pineywoods*			
Randall Lineback*			
White Park			

Goats

San Clemente (F)*	Nigerian Dwarf	Oberhasli	Brush*
			Spanish*
			Tennessee
			Fainting*
			Wooden Leg*

Horses

Akhal-Teke	Clydesdale	Friesian	
American Cream*	Dartmoor	Gotland	
Canadian*	Lipizzan	Hackney	
Cleveland Bay	Spanish Mustang/	Shire	
Exmoor	Spanish Barb*		
Rocky Mountain*			
Sable Island (F)*			
Suffolk Punch			

Sheep

Cotswold	Clun Forest	Black Welsh	Barbados*
Gulf Coast Native*	Delaine Merino	Mountain	Boricua*
Hog Island (F)*	Karakul	Dorset Horn	
Leicester	Katahdin*	Jacob	
Longwool	Lincoln	North Country	
Santa Cruz (F)*	Navajo Churro*	Cheviot	
Wiltshire Horn	St. Croix*	Oxford	
	Tunis*	Shetland	

Swine

Gloucester Old Spot	Hereford*	Tamworth	Guinea Hog*
Large Black			Mulefoot*
Ossabaw Island (F)*			Red Wattle*
Saddleback			

* = Unique to North America
(F) = Feral population or breed of feral origin

Section III

Recommendations for Livestock Genetic Conservation

Chapter 14

Recommendations

$\mathbf{B}$ased on the analysis of the data which have been gathered in this census, several recommendations have emerged to support conservation of livestock breeds. Additional documentation is needed for the genetic resources held in public collections of livestock and poultry. Expanded breed characterizations are needed to better match genetic ability to a wider array of production programs, and additional study of livestock use and potential is needed. Conservation efforts are necessary in both the public and private sectors and should include protection of both live animals and preserved genetic material. Livestock conservation should be viewed as an emerging international issue.

1. Expand Research and Evaluation of North American Livestock

Breed Status

A first step toward any conservation program is the evaluation of the present situation. The purpose of the current census is to evaluate the status of genetic diversity in the North American livestock species. There are three elements necessary to this evaluation: numerical status, genetic status, and context of use within agriculture, which in effect is a breed's habitat. The North American Livestock Census presented here includes each of the above elements, as well as an exploration of the overall status of each species relative to genetic diversity.

Two other research projects are urgently needed to complete the task at hand: 1) an inventory of public collections of live animals and genetic holdings, and 2) an inventory of poultry stocks held in public collections and in private ownership.

Inventory of Public Collections: The land grant colleges have traditionally been the sites of extensive livestock and poultry collections, including live animal herds and flocks and genetic holdings (such as semen, embryos, and DNA). In lean economic times, many of these collections — particularly dairy cattle herds and poultry flocks — are being eliminated by the stroke of a pen without regard to their value or the wider implications of their loss.

A national inventory of public collections should be conducted immediately as a way to identify unique populations. The need for this inventory is urgent, since many livestock and poultry science programs are being eliminated. At the same time, a survey should be conducted of unpublished research pertaining to breed characteristics, some of which may provide data relevant to current livestock production problems.

The United States Department of Agriculture (USDA) is to be congratulated for the establishment of a national livestock database as part of an ambitious livestock conservation program. The database will operate within the Genetic Resources Information Network (GRIN) now in use for plant genetic resources and will maintain current information on breed populations and characteristics. Information will be provided to the agricultural community, to the public, and to international data banks.

Agriculture Canada has begun a livestock conservation program at the Ottawa Agriculture Center. This program will include breed characterization, a data bank, and a collection of genetic materials and live animals. Cooperative effort between USDA and Agriculture Canada will insure that the data systems are mutually accessible.

Inventory of Poultry Stocks: Dr. Ralph Soames of the University of Connecticut developed an exhaustive directory of public poultry collections; the directory is now managed by Dr. James Bitgood at the University of Wisconsin. Unfortunately, university poultry flocks, as well as several of the poultry science departments which once maintained these collections, are disappearing. Public collections are held in public trust and must not be casually discarded without inventory and evaluation.

The loss of genetic diversity within the poultry industry is now being recognized. The Agricultural Research Service of USDA is responding to this concern by increasing the level of research on genetic characterization and gene mapping, as well as focusing on the establishment and maintenance of reference poultry flocks. This effort should be expanded to include all production stocks of the poultry species.

In 1987 the American Livestock Breeds Conservancy conducted a survey of poultry breeds held by seasonal hatcheries. The startling results were published in the 1987 *Poultry Census and Sourcebook*. Many breeds which had formerly played a significant part in poultry production were discovered to be existing in limited numbers. An evaluation of breeding stocks at seasonal hatcheries is necessary to determine the actual number and character of genetic stocks held in private hands.

Breed Characterization

Agricultural research has paid relatively little attention to livestock breed characterization. No one assumes that a single variety of grain or grass will provide optimum returns in every climate, production method, or use. The same is true of livestock breeds. Livestock breed characteristics have not been matched to the changing needs or different environments of production. Instead, we have selected for uniformity in our livestock and uniformity in our livestock production systems.

Breed characteristics, once documented, can be the basis of expanded opportunity in the livestock industry. For example, Highland cattle were historically adapted to a cold, wet climate and rough forage, and thrive under those conditions today. The climate of the Caribbean and the need for meat, not wool, shaped the characteristics of the Barbados, St. Croix, and other hair sheep, which have a high degree of parasite resistance. Breed specific research to compare parasite resistance, forage efficiency, and other qualities of interest to the livestock industry is the best way to tap genetic diversity for current use.

The Sustainable Agriculture Research and Education (SARE) program of the USDA can assist in this effort through the recognition and reward of livestock projects which include elements of genetic conservation. The documentation of breed use in projects which are both agriculturally innovative and agriculturally productive would significantly add to current knowledge about livestock on diversified farms. The selection of breeds which have regional adaptation, forage efficiency, and niche market potential should be encouraged. Genetic diversity must be used for it to enhance the quality of rural life.

Characterization of the broadest variety of livestock breeds is a powerful complement to the livestock genome mapping projects directed by USDA, which have as a goal the description of species at the genetic level. More knowledge about individual breeds enhances opportunities for identification and use of diversity within each species.

In particular need of breed characterization are landrace and feral breeds, which have been shaped through natural as well as human selection and may show unique genetic traits. Evaluation is necessary to determine if these are indeed distinct breeds. Of highest priority are those domestic populations which have historical documentation, including Florida Cracker and Pineywoods cattle, Gulf Coast Native sheep, Caribbean hair sheep, Spanish goats, myotonic goats, and Guinea hogs.

Relatively few feral livestock populations are of genetic interest, as the majority are recent in origin and of crossbred ancestry. While feral animals undoubtedly can cause great damage to fragile ecological systems, these same unique environments have often exerted dramatic selection pressures resulting in animals with specific and unusual genetic adaptations. Policies should be implemented for lands coming into public or private conservation management to include a survey of all species of animals on the properties. Feral livestock present should be evaluated to determine genetic significance prior to extermination; those stocks which are potentially significant should be conserved, either *in situ* or *ex situ*.

Livestock Use and Potential

Researchers need to go beyond an evaluation of feed conversion to consider a wider range of performance characteristics. Of particular importance is research on livestock in low-input production systems. This research should include relevant breed characteristics, such as reproductive efficiency, parasite and disease resistance, and longevity; as well as the use of livestock in such agricultural services as waste recycling, pest control, and land improvement.The Cooperative Extension Service and the Cooperative State Research Service, in conjunction with the land grant colleges, must take the lead.

Sustainable agriculture organizations, which now sponsor a growing network of on-farm research projects, should expand their research integrating livestock management with crop production. This research should include breed specific evaluation. No single breed or species of animals is equally able to meet every production criterion. It is likely that livestock performance under sustainable systems can be improved through the use of breeds which have genetic potentials more appropriate to those systems.

2. Conserve Breeds to Protect Genetic Diversity

The genetic diversity within livestock species is best protected through the conservation of a variety of distinct breeds. A comprehensive conservation program should assure that each breed is not only numerically strong but genetically healthy. This can be accomplished through complementary forms of conservation — live animal conservation and the cryogenic preservation of genetic materials, such as semen, embryos, and DNA. Live animal conservation ensures that the breeds will be used and continue to evolve to meet climatic and market changes. The freezing of semen and embryos is not a replacement for the maintenance of live animals, but does serve as a useful addition to live animal programs. Frozen genetic materials can be preserved and reintroduced into the breed in the future.

Live Animal Conservation: Private Efforts

The use of livestock breeds is essential to their conservation. A variety of agricultural systems is necessary to the conservation of a variety of breeds. This can include working historical farms, agricultural research programs, and commercial enterprises. Agricultural systems are the habitat of domestic breeds. As museum pieces, breeds will certainly become extinct.

At the heart of live animal conservation are private agricultural efforts. Individual farmers and breeders have already saved numerous breeds from extinction.

Support for private efforts has come in many different forms. The Cooperative Extension Service has offices in nearly every county and is an excellent source of animal husbandry information and advice. The Service, however, must expand what it has to offer about the range of breeds and their characteristics, and about livestock uses, production systems, and marketing options in order to truly support genetic conservation.

Of greatest need for most breeders is technical information on breeding for genetic conservation. The American Livestock Breeds Conservancy operates a technical support program to educate breeders about the needs and methods of conservation breeding, including ways to develop detailed conservation breeding programs for individual herds. The urgency and complexity of these programs increases as breed numbers decrease. The breeders of the rarer breeds need much more support and information than do those of the more common breeds.

Sustainable agriculture organizations are beginning to recognize the vital relationship between livestock and crops in integrated diversified farming and so explore both new and traditional ways to utilize animals. These organizations can provide valuable information about livestock management and, as breed specific research is generated, this information will gradually become more specific and even more useful. An excellent source of information is the Appropriate Technology Transfer for Rural Areas (ATTRA) in Fayetteville, Arkansas.

Breed associations exist to promote livestock breeds. While they actually share the common ground of promoting registered purebred livestock, many breed associations seem to consider each other as competitors rather than as colleagues. Stronger inter-association networks could strengthen the work of all individuals and associations. The increased availability of information, ideas, and innovations would promote the wonderful array of pure breeds and allow the associations to serve their own constituencies better. The National Pedigreed Livestock Council is an example of an organization well suited to enhance inter-association dialogue by fostering an inclusive philosophy that reaches out to breed associations of all sizes.

Live Animal Conservation: Public Efforts

There is historical precedent for a government role in conservation. The Texas Longhorn was saved from extinction by Congressional order, with herds maintained at federal expense on federal lands. The state of Florida has initiated programs to conserve the Florida Cracker, its historic breed of cattle.

Public policy can be improved to conserve breed resources in concert with the private sector. The USDA's Agricultural Research Service should maintain and study a wider variety of livestock breeds. The USDA Meat Animal Research Center (MARC) is an excellent example of the possibilities. MARC is now utilizing twenty-six breeds of beef cattle in production studies and genome mapping. Sheep and swine research should also include a wider range of breeds and production systems. Broadening research to evaluate pure breed characteristics in differing production systems would improve understanding of species potential.

Publicly supported institutions, including zoos, nature centers, agricultural museums, historic sites, and demonstration farms can also contribute to live animal conservation through the maintenance and promotion of heritage breeds of livestock. At living history farms and agricultural museums the use of historically accurate breeds is as essential to interpretation as is the use of historically accurate buildings, tools, and clothing. Visitors are spellbound watching Devon oxen at work, Cotswold fleece being shorn, an Ossabaw Island sow and piglets rooting in a woodland, or American Cream Draft horses pulling a stately carriage.

In many parts of North America, specific breeds of livestock have played a significant role in economic and historic development. These breeds are necessary for an accurate and complete historic interpretation of the past. The Texas Longhorn and the Florida Cracker cattle, for example, were the basis of regional agriculture for a succession of cultures. Navajo Churro sheep transformed the cultures of the Southwest. Vermont Merino sheep supplied wool for the mills of the newly industrialized nineteenth century New England. The Canadian horse was the first horse breed developed in North America and influenced the development of other North American horse breeds.

An example of the marriage of conservation with public education can be found at Colonial Williamsburg, an historic site depicting life in 1770s Virginia. Leicester Longwool sheep were the best modern example of colonial sheep, yet they have been extinct in North America since the middle of this century. Colonial Williamsburg has re-imported the breed for its own use and developed a conservation breeding program to maximize genetic diversity in this population, which is globally threatened. Many endangered breeds could profit by similar support programs at other historic sites.

Cryogenic Preservation

In addition to live animal collections, genetic materials — semen, embryos, and DNA — must also be protected for the future. Modern technology enables these genetic materials to be frozen for an indefinite period, then thawed and used to reproduce offspring which reflect the genetics of the donor. In the strictest sense, this is "preservation" since it preserves materials as they were without any evolution or change. A genetically diverse collection of materials in storage may be reintroduced to a living population in the future as a way to expand numbers or genetic breadth. The preserved genetic material may also serve as a research baseline to evaluate changes which have taken place.

The technology for collecting semen and embryos from cattle and storing them in liquid nitrogen is now widely utilized. Bull semen from the earliest collections fifty years ago is still fertile. This means that these bulls, though long dead, can still contribute to contemporary breeding programs. While artificial insemination and long term storage of genetic materials in other species has lagged somewhat behind cattle, the technology for successful assisted reproduction is progressing rapidly.

Cryogenic preservation should have as its goal the collection and maintenance of a representative stock of genetic materials for each species. Even those breeds without current market favor still warrant collection if this strategy is to serve its purpose.

We recommend the establishment of national livestock gene banks to store genetic materials for future reference and use. Such a national bank would not be expensive to operate and could easily be accomplished within current national agriculture policies. The cryogenic banking of a representative sample of all North American breeds could have a profound impact on the long-term conservation of livestock genetic diversity.

3. Increase Public Understanding and Support for Agricultural Diversity

Farmers make up just two percent of the United States population, but since everyone eats, everyone has a stake in agriculture. As the increased uniformity of agricultural products is part of the cause of genetic erosion, an increased appreciation of diversity in food products and production systems is part of the solution.

119

The public must increase its support for a variety of commodities and a variety of production methods of the animal products and services which so enrich our lives. The growth of interest in foods produced as "grass fed," "organic," and through other sustainable methods can strengthen the market niche for a variety of breeds and thus for genetic diversity.

Animals also provide an amazing array of fibers to keep us warm and to delight our senses. Fashion mavens and fiber crafters have recognized the unusual textures from Cotswold and Karakul fleeces, and the array of colors from Jacob, Shetland, and Black Welsh Mountain sheep. This interest has in turn invigorated the interest of spinners and weavers in heritage breeds.

The market for breed-specific products must continue to grow. In the past, Golden Guernsey milk enjoyed a premier spot in the market. Certified Angus beef is trademarked, and limited label approval has been granted for Highland beef and Churro lamb. Elsie the Borden cow has been a corporate symbol for 57 years. After a 20 year retirement, the aging but still beautiful Jersey cow recently appeared in Times Square at the unveiling of a new Borden advertising campaign.

Sites focusing on public education are making significant efforts to remedy our national agricultural illiteracy. Two noteworthy examples are Lake Farmpark, a county park near Cleveland, Ohio, and Mount Vernon, Virginia, the home of George Washington which has an ambitious new agriculture program. These are models to which other institutions can turn for agricultural education outreach.

Environmental foundations have an important role to play in genetic conservation. Funders of biodiversity issues have been narrow in their understanding of this issue, and they need to realize that biodiversity is not confined to North American old growth forests or tropical rainforests. Instead, biodiversity is a necessary and integral part of all biological systems, including agriculture. In addition, some environmental funders have held a narrow understanding of agriculture — the human occupation with the longest and most widespread effect on the environment. Agriculture is far more diverse than may be realized, and within it lie the seeds of environmentally friendly food and fiber production systems. Support for such agricultural systems would produce great benefits for environmental and genetic conservation.

4. Develop Corporate Support for Genetic Conservation

The corporate sector, particularly the food industry, has benefitted from the genetic diversity at the heart of North American agricultural success. Industry has a moral obligation to protect this genetic heritage as well as a vested interest in preserving this resource to meet its own future needs.

"Green marketing" is already proving profitable and effective. Products with a breed identity already have a proven record which is waiting to be expanded. Bull Durham tobacco, Coleman's mustard, James Hanley beer, and many other products have been sold with the aid of breed specific mascots. The Anheuser Busch Clydesdale horses are one of the best known and loved corporate symbols in history. Less well known is the generous support that the Anheuser Busch has given to the Clydesdale breed, particularly when it neared extinction in the 1950s and 1960s. As the public becomes reacquainted with an agricultural heritage, breed specific marketing and conservation will become even more successful. Certainly, the return of Elsie the cow must be seen as a positive move.

5. Increase International Cooperation

Most of the countries of Europe, as well as India, China, and Brazil, have moved to establish state or private livestock conservation programs. These vary in scope and ambition from a semen collection of indigenous cattle breeds in France to a comprehensive genetic conservation effort in Switzerland that includes livestock, vegetables, fruits, and grains. These efforts not only enjoy government support but the interest of the public. The shared interest in conservation of

Figure 14.1. Clydesdale stallion.

our respective national genetic treasures is a source of international goodwill and mutual benefit.

Rare Breeds International (RBI), a non-governmental organization, was formed in 1991 to serve as an umbrella agency for public and private livestock conservation organizations from around the world. The American Livestock Breeds Conservancy is a founding member. International livestock data banks are in operation in Hanover, Germany, and Rome, Italy. A priority for RBI will be the development of conservation plans for breeds found in more than one nation. This will be of great benefit to North Americans, since many breeds found here are international in distribution.

Import/export regulations now present a formidable barrier to the exchange of genetic materials around the world. Regulations have generally been established as barriers to disease, but some are outdated and serve primarily as an obstacle to exchange. Research must be encouraged to develop a wider range of diagnostic procedures to screen infected animals and methods for the safe international transfer of disease-free genetic materials.

Conclusions

Genetic diversity, as represented by animals and plants from around the world, has been essential to the success of modern agriculture. Conservation of this diversity is critical to the future.

Livestock genetic diversity is demonstrated visually in breed distinctions such as color, size, and conformation and in each breed's unique abilities, behaviors, and characteristics. A diversity of breeds within each livestock species makes possible the integral role of animals in agriculture. The use of livestock services and products continues the historic human-animal partnership which has been characteristic of agriculture in every culture around the world.

Throughout history, agriculturalists have been stewards of the genetic legacy to be passed on to succeeding generations. The present generation threatens to bankrupt the inheritance, leaving little to those who follow. What took centuries to develop can be lost in our lifetime. If lost, it cannot be recreated. Only a renewed commitment to stewardship by our generation will protect the genetic legacy for the future.

Appendixes

Appendix I

Case Studies of Livestock Extinction

Improvement in the Marketplace
An Economic History of the United States Livestock Industry and the Demise of Historic Breeds of Cattle, Sheep, and Swine

Bruce Kalk
Southern Connecticut University, New Haven, CT

There is an intrinsically close relationship between the history of food habits, the economic development of the livestock industry, and the rise and fall of specific livestock breeds. What could be more enlightening to the conservation of present breeds than the case studies of past extinctions?

An underlying theme to the historical developments taking place in North American livestock has been the transformation of the art of animal breeding to the science of mass production. This transformation was dependent upon three developments in science and American economic history: first, the mid-nineteenth century emergence of the marketplace mindset, as farmers ceased to produce for their households and towns and began instead to produce for fickle consumers in distant places.[1] Second, the modern field of genetics arose with the rediscovery of Mendel's work on biologically-inherited traits in peas. The third development was the emergence of a culture of consumer-based mass capitalism by the 1920s.[2]

Signs of the transformation in livestock can be seen in the 1930s and 1940s. In 1937, for example, the International Association of Milk Sanitarians began publishing the *Journal of Milk Technology* for the dairy industry. Five years later, the American Society of Animal Producers began publishing its *Journal of Animal Science*. The latter clearly set the tone for the scientific output-oriented direction that livestock production as an industry was taking.[3] In fact, during the 1930s, agricultural journals emphasized breeds and breeding less and instead referred increasingly to profit maximizing approaches to livestock raising.[4]

This transformation led to the extinction of livestock breeds no longer deemed profitable. Some breeds were lost as a result of cross-breeding for improvement; others because of the agricultural decline of one region of the country. The change in consumer taste and preferences accounted for other extinctions. Some breeds that could exist well with minimal care and feeding became extinct because their sturdiness failed to lend itself to maximum output. In the end, each of these extinct breeds is lost to future generations.

Cattle

The history of American cattle breed extinctions is surprisingly obscured by confusion over breed names. It is often difficult to determine if cattle which have been lost from the record were true breeds which became extinct, breeds which merged with others, breeds which simply underwent a name change, or transient populations which never were breeds to begin with.

An example of this confusion is the case of the Alderney cow. Alderney, Jersey, and Guernsey make up the three Channel Islands located between England and France. Each island was known historically for its own dairy cattle breed. While the Guernsey and Jersey breeds are still widely known, the Alderney is globally extinct. An effort was made to trace the breed's history and extinction in North America, but the task proved fruitless. Instead, there is ample evidence that in the United States, the term "Alderney" was "indiscriminately applied to the cattle of all the islands of the little British group called the Channel Islands."[5] While we know there are no more Alderney cattle, it is impossible to be sure how many there once were or how the loss of the term in North America is related to the global demise of a particular population of cattle.

However, research does show clear evidence of the extinction of some other cattle breeds. The Yellow Dane, for example, was lost during the late eighteenth century.[6] The Polled Albion, developed in the late nineteenth century, is no longer found. Though never widely known, this breed did have a breed association registering purebreds.[7] About 1900, writers discussed the Holdnerness and, to a lesser extent, the Teeswater. These were likely types of Shorthorns, but at some point the names ceased to be applied. Whether that indicates the demise of a bona fide animal breed, however, is unclear.[8] It is probable that they were absorbed into the Shorthorn breed.

The extinctions of two important North American cattle breeds — the Polled Durham and the Kerry — are better documented. The Polled Durham was a type of Shorthorn, developed from purebreds and from muley (polled) cows.[9] The Ohio State Board of Agriculture awarded this strain of cattle its first official recognition as a breed. Polled Durhams were shown at the Ohio Centennial and State Fair in 1888. The breed won numerous prizes at state and county fairs during the late nineteenth century.[10] Polled Durhams produced more milk than Shorthorns and thus became increasingly popular in the United States toward the turn of the century, particularly in Indiana, Illinois, Ohio, and Texas.[11] Breeders organized the American Polled Durham Breeders Association in 1889 and published a herdbook.[12] The Association proudly alluded to the economic and social benefits of the breed, which as hornless cattle spared many farmhands the injuries commonly associated with horns or their removal.[13] It is unclear why breeders ultimately lost interest in the Polled Durham, but the herdbook was last published in 1918. By the end of World War II, the breed had become extinct by assimilation into the gene pool of the Shorthorn.[14]

A second cattle breed, the Kerry, has also become extinct in North America. The Kerry was imported from Ireland as early as 1824.[15] Importations continued until mid-century, but even then the Kerry were never geographically widespread in the United States.[16] Nevertheless, the breed attracted sufficient attention here; the *Kerry and Dexter Herdbook* was first published in 1898. The American Kerry and Dexter Cattle Society organized in 1911.[17]

The Kerry was a particularly docile animal, but more importantly, produced a fair amount of milk on even "the coarsest cattle-food."[18] The Kerry was "the poor man's cow; hardy, living everywhere, yielding, for her size, abundance of milk of good quality."[19] Although the breed did thrive in adverse conditions, it produced in general only a moderate amount of milk.[20] The Kerry's inability to compete with other breeds under better conditions may indeed explain why the animal failed to survive in the United States.

Today, the Kerry is critically endangered worldwide, with the primary populations in Ireland and Britain. A few Kerries have been reimported to North America and are of particular interest to historic sites.

Sheep

It is a single irony of the American sheep industry that as it came of age, the progenitor of modern sheep breeding — the Leicester Longwool — was lost. The story of the American sheep industry is the tale of the Leicester and of the Merino, two breeds which fared very differently during the past two hundred years.

Some background on the sheep industry is relevant to the breed histories. While the British have made a great success of raising sheep in Great Britain and nearly everywhere else they have been — Australia, New Zealand, and South Africa — sheep have never been of great agricultural importance in the United States.[21] Americans do not eat much mutton or lamb; in fact, lamb consumption has hovered around seven pounds a year, in contrast with beef and pork consumption, which were each about ten times as great.[22] Toward the end of the nineteenth century lamb did become somewhat more popular, especially among immigrants used to its taste, but this development did not permanently alter the unfavorable position of lamb in the United States.

The other economic function of sheep — wool production — might well have made the industry more successful in the United States, but American consumers have generally imported their wool from abroad instead.[23] This may be due to the cyclic nature of the wool market. This has discouraged the development of a strong domestic industry in favor of imports from Australia and New Zealand, where wool is far cheaper to produce.

One of the first breeds of sheep brought to North America was the Leicester Longwool (also called the English Leicester). The Leicester was developed in England in the late eighteenth century by Robert Bakewell, known as the father of modern animal breeding and scientific improvement of livestock. The breed was known for its long, lustrous fleece and its large frame.

Figure I.1. Leicester Longwool ram.

The Leicester Longwool arrived in North America before the American Revolution, and George Washington purchased Leicesters for Mount Vernon. The breed was highly prized, especially for its value in cross-breeding, and spread in popularity in the United States in the earliest part of the nineteenth century.[24] Its coarse fleece was used for blankets, coats, and other garments where strength, warmth, and long wear were necessary.

Another of the earliest sheep imports to the New World was the Merino sheep, which came from Spain. Merinos were known across Europe and existed in different varieties, or sub-breeds. Several varieties were imported to the United States, beginning in the eighteenth century. When Merinos were imported to the United States, however, the many varieties were reconsolidated into a breed termed the "American Merino."[25] The Merino was highly prized for the excellence of its fine fleece,[26] soft enough to be used for underwear, and its popularity stemmed from the movement toward fine woolen fleece.[27]

During the eighteenth century, Great Britain was the major supplier of woolen goods to the British colonies. However, with the outbreak of the War of 1812, Great Britain abruptly ceased exports to the United States. The result was a dearth of fine wool and a dramatic interest in the American Merino breed that came to be known as the "Merino Craze." The price of Merino sheep and wool went through the roof. Before the war broke out, one pound of Merino wool brought 75 cents. By 1813, a pound of the same wool was worth two to three dollars.[28] When the war ended in 1815, the trade in imported woolens resumed and the Merino Craze was over. The sheep returned to their prewar market value, but many speculators had lost their fortunes on Merinos.

The Merino sheep had come to eclipse the Leicester during the "Merino Craze." Although prices for the breed dropped after the war, interest in it remained strong until the the Panic of 1837, which brought a complete collapse in the market for fine woolens.[29] The result was a turning away from the fine wooled Merino[30] toward meat type sheep[31] and toward the medium wool fleece breeds, as the price of this fleece had held steadier during the depression. These changes favored the Leicester Longwool as a large framed breed used for meat as well as fleece. The breed was back in vogue in the 1840s, particularly on the eastern seaboard.

The Merino remained popular in the West, significant as the sheep industry (indeed agriculture itself) was moving westward[32] to take advantage of cheap and plentiful grazing on the open range.[33] In 1840, the nine northeastern states of New England, New York, New Jersey, and Pennsylvania produced 56.6 percent of all American sheep; by 1860, they produced only 27.4 percent.[34] By the late 1850s, eastern sheep producers could scarcely compete with westerners. It cost one to two dollars per head to raise sheep in Pennsylvania, but only twenty-five to fifty cents per head in parts of the Midwest.[35] As American sheep-raising moved west, the breed of choice in the western livestock ranges was the Merino. Thus the Merino was prospering where sheep were on the rise; it had fallen out of favor only in the East, where sheep-raising itself was on the decline.[36]

The Leicester also had the disadvantage of characteristics which did not match current market demands. Its meat was considered poor quality; it was not only fatty, but the fat was not mixed with the meat itself but deposited in a layer around the meat. The second problem for the Leicester was, ironically, also its main attraction: its characteristic long, coarse fleece, which began to lose favor with American consumers,[37] who came to prefer medium and fine wool. Sheep-raising was highly competitive. Once producers had a market-oriented mindset, they saw the Leicester as a relatively unattractive and un-profitable breed.

This is not to say that the Leicester was doomed by the middle of the nineteenth century. The American Leicester Breeders' Association was formed in 1888 and registered over 15,000 purebreds between 1888 and 1914.[38] The breed was seen as excellent for cross-breeding for the production of market lambs. It did spread west, and by the turn of the twentieth century was found in Pennsylvania, Michigan, Illinois, Iowa, Nebraska, and Oregon in the United States and in Ontario in Canada.[39] Yet, gradually, the Leicester's use in cross-breed-ing resulted in its loss. The animal was bred to improve other stocks to such an extent that as early as 1914 one writer commented that there were probably no purebreds in existence.[40] The American Leicester Breeders' Association continued in operation, though by 1930 it was estimated that only 213 registered purebreds were left.[41] It is safe to say that the animal became extinct in the United States shortly there-after.

The Leicester Longwool has been re-imported from Tasmania for historic interpretation at Colonial Williamsburg Foundation in Virginia. A conservation breeding program is underway to reestablish the United States population. Since the breed is globally endangered, this effort is of importance and also serves as a powerful reminder of the earlier extinction of the American Leicester Longwool.

Swine

A complete transformation took place in the swine industry be-tween the early nineteenth century, when hogs were kept for house-hold consumption, and the mid-twentieth century, when hogs were produced as a commodity for distant markets. The transformation was marked by a consolidation of breeds, a mania for crossbreeding, and the displacement of the "older" agricultural regions by the West. Co-incident was the extinction of a number of historic breeds of swine. In fact, most of the documented cases of livestock extinction in North America involve swine breeds.

Two waves of swine extinctions took place. The first wave occurred during the mid-nineteenth century and resulted in the loss of several improved American breeds. These include the Byfield hog and the Irish Grazier, probably one of the two most popular breeds in the South during this period.[42]

The second wave of extinctions occurred during the mid-twenti-eth century and included three popular swine breeds commonly men-tioned in livestock manuals one hundred years ago. The Davis Victoria, Cheshire, and Essex hog had each attracted interest among swine-breeders during the late nineteenth century; today no herds survive.[43]

It is important to note that at the turn of the century, registrations of each of these breeds exceeded those of the Hampshire hog, now the third most popular breed in the United States.[44]

Evolution of the Swine Industry

What ultimately forms the marketplace for livestock are the changing food habits of the consumers. Of course, these habits are themselves the products of sweeping societal forces, such as the exposure to new cultures, or the availability of transportation, or even the inertia of market forces themselves. The literature on American food habits indicates two revolutionary changes taking place which affected the development of the swine industry. The first was the decline of pork relative to other meats. During the early nineteenth century, domestic consumption of pork was astronomical. Yet this pork preference shifted considerably in favor of beef over the course of the nineteenth and twentieth centuries. As a result, the ratio of the hog population to the human population in the United States has declined steadily since 1840.[45] Increased competition has been characteristic of the effort to satisfy the demands of a marketplace less and less hungry for pork. As a result, breeds which could be even marginally competitive surpassed others.

The second change that took place in American food habits was the decreasing demand for fatty meats. Part of this trend manifested itself in a decreasing demand for lard per se, particularly with competition from vegetable fats and oils. Another aspect of this trend, however, was the transition away from the extremely fatty meats preferred in the nineteenth century toward leaner cuts of pork.[46] Eating habits had therefore changed in two directions: away from pork towards other meats and away from lard-type hogs toward bacon-type hogs. The lard breeds were either selected for greater leanness or became extinct. Generally, those breeds which were already most common (such as the Poland China) were those which received the most active selection to meet changing market demands, while other breeds were left behind.

Food habits were not the only thing that changed, however. The hog industry, propelled by the extension of railroads deep into the American interior, moved geographically to the north and west over time. As early as 1810, there were economic advantages to hog production in the "West." Farmers in New York's Mohawk River Valley lost out to those in western New York; both were then displaced by midwestern hog producers.[47] The abundant production of corn and its usefulness as feed for swine firmly linked the corn belt to hog raising. As corn prices rose, the price differential grew wider; it became cheaper to raise hogs within the corn belt, and increasingly expensive to raise them farther away. The plentiful supply of cheap land in the

Midwest added to its benefits for hog-raising.[48] The development of railroads made possible the transportation of swine to packing centers and, thereafter, to distant markets.

By 1840, hog-raising centered in Kentucky, Ohio, and Indiana. That year, not quite 17 percent of United States hogs were raised in New England and the mid-Atlantic states; by 1860, hog production in the same northeastern states had declined to only 7.5 percent of the United States total.[49] It was simply impossible, during the mid-nineteenth century, for easterners to compete when their cost of producing pork was 6 cents per pound as compared to 2–2½ cents per pound in the Midwest.[50]

The period after the Civil War saw a continuation of the trend. Between 1850 and 1910, the total number of swine in New York state declined by over a third while the state's population increased sharply. The hog belt continued to move even farther north and west, reaching into the northern great plains states.[51] By the mid-twentieth century, the Midwest had almost completely displaced the Northeast in hog production.

The developments outlined above all had an impact on the hog-raising industry. In particular they led to the rise and fall of several breeds of hogs.

The First Wave of Extinctions: Nineteenth Century

A "first wave" of swine breed extinctions occurred between 1835 and 1900, affecting some of the first improved breeds that had been introduced to the United States in the beginning of the nineteenth century. Among them was the Bedford, variously called the Cumberland, the Bedfordshire, or (in New York and Massachusetts) the Woburn hog.[52] This breed first came to the United States in the late eighteenth century when the Duke of Bedford sent some of his hogs to George Washington.[53] The Bedford hog was widely distributed in the United States during the early nineteenth century, especially in Maryland, Pennsylvania, Delaware, and Virginia. It was also known in Massachusetts[54] and in New York.

The Bedford was considered a significant improver of common stock. It was noted to exhibit a "distinctly refining influence" on the common hogs of Chester County, Pennsylvania, resulting in the establishment of a new breed, the Chester White.[55] But the Bedford itself did not survive. One writer remarked in 1855 that "our hogs have been crossed upon the 'Berkshire,' 'Irish Grazier,' 'Woburn,' &c., until we scarcely know what we have, except that they are hogs."[56] By 1872, the United States Department of Agriculture considered the Bedford already extinct. We can thus date the Bedford's extinction to sometime between 1855–1870.[57]

132

The Byfield hog was another victim of its utility in crossbreeding programs. The Byfield originated in Byfield, Massachusetts, about 1800 when Chester Forham discovered some floppy-eared hogs — allegedly a mix of Bedford, Old English, and Chinese hogs — in a local marketplace. Through his efforts, the Byfield quickly became the predominant breed in New England and emigrated with New Englanders west to Ohio sometime before 1816. There the Byfield hog became one of the base breeds for the development of the Poland China hog. Paradoxically once again, the Byfield, which had been so esteemed, was supplanted by its Poland China offspring and shortly afterward became extinct.[58]

The Irish Grazier was another significant breed that died out after being used to develop a more advantageous animal for a competitive market. During the early nineteenth century, Irish immigrants imported their country's native hogs in very large numbers. The animal was greatly valued for the ability to thrive on pasture, garden, and dairy left-overs alone, with almost no attention. In 1839 the Irish Grazier was introduced to the Miami Valley of Ohio, where it became an element in the development of the Poland China breed.[59]

Although the Irish Grazier was criticized for being slow-maturing and big boned, it remained one of the two or three most popular breeds throughout the country. It was extremely popular in the South on the eve of the Civil War.[60] The Irish Grazier is not mentioned in livestock literature around 1900, however, so it apparently disappeared between 1870–1900.

"There might be pages of testimony given in favor of Suffolks," wrote the United States Commissioner of Agriculture of one of the country's most widespread hog breeds in 1863. "We think it no exaggeration to say that we believe three-fourths of the hogs of northern Illinois have strains of Suffolk blood."[61] The Suffolk, the Irish Grazier, and Berkshire were probably the three most popular swine breeds in the United States during the 1850s.[62] Farmers praised the Suffolk for keeping easier, maturing younger, and fattening quicker with less expense than other breeds.[63] But the nineteenth century proved to be the heyday of the Suffolk. By the twentieth century, the breed was no longer regularly mentioned in livestock manuals. In 1930, only 303 living registered pure-bred Suffolks existed. The Suffolk seems to have disappeared thereafter.[64]

Also of significance during the nineteenth century was the Big China hog, considered to be the forerunner of the Poland China breed.[65] John Wallace, a trustee of the Shaker Society, visited Philadelphia in 1816 and procured several of these swine, which he brought back to southwestern Ohio. The agricultural periodicals *Ohio Cultivator* and *Western Farmer* frequently lauded the virtues of the Big China for crossbreeding purposes.[66] By 1835, the animal became known as the "War-

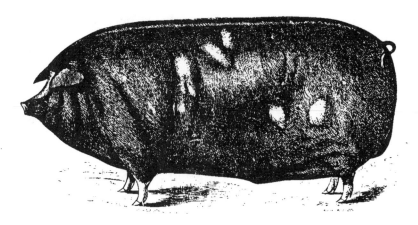

Figure I.2. Poland China boar.

ren County hog;" when crossed with the Bedford, Byfield, Russian, and (later) the Berkshire hog, it became known as the Poland China.[67]

We know nothing of the history of a number of breeds, including the Russian hog so important to the development of the Poland China. The same can be said of the Siamese, Calcutta, Barnitz, Lincoln, Middlesex, and Newbury White breeds.

The last part of the "first wave" of breed extinctions concerns several red hog breeds and types known in New York, New England, and the mid-Atlantic during the late colonial period. These included Guinea hogs from West Africa which arrived in America beginning in 1804 with the slave trade; red Spanish and Portugese hogs imported by Henry Clay beginning in the 1830s; and the ill-defined "native" hogs. Generally these red hogs intermixed on a local basis and were not considered "improved" animals; in many areas, local red hog stock was a conglomerate of several ancestors distinctive primarily in geographic terms.[68]

The recognition of two particular red hog strains, however, paved the way for the establishment of a single recognized red hog breed towards the end of the century. Saratoga County, New York, saw the foundation stock for its "Duroc" strain of hogs develop during the 1820s. Meanwhile, in 1857, James B. Lyman, agricultural editor for the New York *Tribune*, made reference to the "Jersey Red," and thus christened New Jersey's red hog stock a swine breed.

These two breeds, the Duroc and Jersey Red, were formally united in 1872 at the National Swine Breeders' Convention. In 1883, the Duroc-Jersey Record Association was formed. The breed attracted considerable attention and as it flourished, it absorbed nearly all other strains of red hogs. It may thus be said that the "extinction" of the individual varieties of red hogs in America was remarkably official, with the establishment of the American Duroc-Jersey Record Association in 1883.[69]

The Second Wave of Extinctions: Early Twentieth Century

The "second wave" of extinctions took place during the first half of the twentieth century when four breeds disappeared: the Essex, the Cheshire, the Curtis Victoria, and the Davis Victoria.

The Essex pig, which probably shared a common ancestor with the American Hampshire, was a popular English swine breed that was first imported to the United States in 1820.[70] Early on, the animal was used more for household rather than for commodity production. The Essex was known to mature early, to grow well off a small amount of food, and possess a high percentage of fat in its meat. At least one farm manual recommended the Essex as a preferred breed for those with a "desire to realize the largest profits with the least outlay of time and money."[71]

The American Essex Association organized and began publishing herdbooks in 1890. Yet shortly afterward, the Essex was clearly in decline. According to one livestock book, the animal's popularity by 1920 had reached "a low ebb...[it is] losing favor year by year," in part because the Essex was judged too fatty, too "delicate," and too often failing to "grow into money."[72] Perceptions about the Essex, as well as growing conditions and market goals, had obviously changed completely during the century since its import.

The Cheshire hog originated in Jefferson County, New York; this "Jefferson County Hog" was first exhibited at the New York State Fair in 1859. Thereafter it became the primary white hog exhibited at New York's fair.[73] The Cheshire was small in size but matured at an extremely early age.[74] A breed association for the Cheshire started in 1884, and in 1905 alone the association registered 1,000 pure-bred hogs. By 1910, the Cheshire was the third-most popular swine breed in New York.[75] Shortly thereafter, however, interest in this particularly docile breed began to wane. The final herdbook was published in 1914.[76]

Although there were Cheshire herds in many parts of the country, the breed remained primarily of interest to breeders in New York state and in Maine, where it represented 3.1 percent and 8.5 percent of the state's hog population, respectively.[77] By 1920, the Cheshire represented 1 percent or less of the hog population outside of the northeastern states. The Cheshire's undoing no doubt stemmed from its regional concentration. By 1930, only forty Cheshire hogs survived; their demise can thus be dated to the 1930s.[78]

The Curtis Victoria pig originated in Lake County, Indiana, about 1850 from the efforts of F. D. Curtis to develop a new breed by crossing a number of existing varieties of improved swine. Curtis hoped to conserve the best genetic qualities of each of the breeds he crossed. The breed failed to catch on, however, and in 1900, after fifty years of history, no known purebreds remained.[79]

Twenty years after Curtis developed his "Victoria" breed, George F. Davis bred Poland Chinas, Chester Whites, Berkshires, and American Suffolks together to produce the Davis Victoria, genetically unrelated to the Curtis breed but also named for the reigning Queen of England.[80] Breeders of the Davis Victoria claimed that the animal shipped well and was extremely resistant to mange and sun-blisters. They also claimed its "unusual economy in production of the flesh."[81] Although a Victoria breed association arose around 1900, the organization apparently did not publish herdbooks. Modern livestock manuals do not discuss the breed at all. As of 1930, only 94 Victoria swine existed. The breed apparently died out shortly thereafter.[82]

The histories of extinct swine breeds demonstrate how market forces and the evolution of food habits affect livestock history. By 1920, over 62 percent of United States swine were estimated to be one of two breeds: the Poland China or the Duroc Jersey.[83] Both of these breeds benefitted from the broad genetic base of several distinct breeds. Ironically, the consolidation of each breed meant the end of most of these distinct founder breeds.

The diversity represented by a wide variety of breeds of swine and other livestock is a genetic treasure chest used extensively in the past to respond to market changes, to develop new breeds, and to emphasize ever different characteristics in the livestock species. Yet modern obsession with short term output alone and the mania for cross-breeding have exacted a toll in breed extinctions. We must look beyond current market needs and profitability to guarantee for the future the same genetic resources we have today. Livestock of the past is not just an historic resource, but an irreplaceable one for the future as well.

---

[1]There has been fascinating historiographical debate on the transformation of the local "household" economy to the market economy. See especially James A. Henretta, "Families and Farms: *Mentalite* in Pre-Industrial America," *William and Mary Quarterly*, 3d ser., 35 (1978), 3–32, and Thomas L. Haskell, "Capitalism and the Rise of the Humanitarian Sensibility," Parts I and II, *American Historical Review* (1985).

[2]A rich literature has arisen discussing this point. See especially Warren I. Susman, *Culture as History: The Transformation of American Society in the Twentieth Century*; Richard W. Fox and T. J. Jackson Lears, eds., *The Culture of Consumption: Critical Essays in American History, 1880–1920*; and Susan Hanson, "Home Sweet Home: Industrialization's Impact on Rural Households, 1865–1925," PhD Dissertation, University of Maryland, 1986.

[3]*Journal of Milk Technology*, 1 (October 1937); *Journal of Animal Science*, 1 (February 1942).

[4]A close scanning of the *Agricultural and Biological Index* amply demonstrates this transition during the 1930s.

⁵William Housman, *Cattle: Breeds and Management* (London, 1905), p. 157. See also A. R. Porter, J. A. Sims, and C. F. Foreman, *Dairy Cattle in American Agriculture* (Ames, Iowa, 1964), p. 37.

⁶James Westfall Thompson, *A History of Livestock Raising in the United States, 1607–1860*, (Washington, DC, 1942), p. 69.

⁷E. V. Wilcox and C. B. Smith, *Farmer's Cyclopedia of Livestock* (New York, 1908). This organization was called the Polled Albion Breeders' Association.

⁸Ibid.

⁹Wilcox and Smith, p. 368.

¹⁰American Polled Durham Breeders' Association, *American Polled Durham Handbook* (Peru, Indiana, 1894–1921), p. xxxix.

¹¹Wilcox and Smith, p. 368.

¹²George W. Curtis, *Horses, Cattle, Sheep and Swine* (New York, 1893), p. 201.

¹³American Polled Durham Breeders' Association, pp. xxxii–xxxv.

¹⁴Interview with Hayes Walker.

¹⁵*American Kerry and Dexter Herdbook* (Columbus, Ohio, 1921), introduction.

¹⁶Ibid. and p. 24.

¹⁷Ibid.

¹⁸Ibid.; Curtis, p. 154.

¹⁹*American Kerry and Dexter Herdbook*, introduction, p. 11.

²⁰Wilcox and Smith, pp. 434–35.

²¹See *USDA Year Book, 1917*, pp. 311–14.

²²Paul W. Chapman and Wayne Dinsmore, *Livestock Farming* (Atlanta, 1953), pp. 388–89; John A. Sims and Leslie E. Johnson, *Animals in the American Economy* (Ames, Iowa, 1972), p. 73.

²³Ibid., pp. 391–92.

²⁴E. L.Shaw and L. L. Heller, "Domestic Breeds of Sheep in America," *Bulletin of the US Department of Agriculture* No. 94, August 17, 1914, pp. 39–42; Charles S. Plumb, *Types and Breeds of Farm Animals* (Boston, 1906).

²⁵There is some dispute as to whether varieties of the Merino constitute "breeds" per se. C. S. Plumb, the noted turn-of-the-century writer on livestock, did not consider the varieties to be separate breeds once they came to America. This includes the Saxon Merino, which originated only twenty-eight years before the first Merino importations to the United States. See Plumb, pp. 339–44.

²⁶John A. Craig, *Sheep-Farming in North America* (New York, 1920), pp. 34, 42–43.

²⁷Percy Wells Bidwell and John I. Falconer, *History of Agriculture in the Northern United States, 1620–1860* (Washington, DC, 1925), p. 410.

²⁸Thompson, p. 80.

²⁹Bidwell and Falconer, p. 407.

³⁰Stevenson Whitcomb Fletcher, *Pennsylvania Agriculture and Country Life, 1640–1840* (Harrisburg, Pennsylvania, 1950), p. 267.

³¹Bidwell and Falconer, p. 410.

³²Bidwell and Falconer, pp. 407–10.

³³This is true even though range areas in the United States were considerably encroached by settlements and grain–growing by the early twentieth century. *USDA Year Book, 1917*, p. 313.

³⁴Bidwell and Falconer, p. 409.

³⁵Fletcher, p. 266.

[36]Bidwell and Falconer, p. 411.

[37]M. S. Ensminger, *Animal Science* (Danville, Illinois, 1983), p. 602; Shaw and Heller, pp. 39–42; and Plumb, pp. 429–436.

[38]Shaw and Heller, p. 42.

[39]Plumb, p. 435.

[40]Shaw and Heller, p. 39.

[41]Henry W. Vaughan, *Types and Market Classes of Livestock* (Columbus, Ohio, 1942), p. 239.

[42]Charles Wayland Towne and Edward Norris Wentworth, *Pigs: From Cave to Corn Belt* (Norman, Oklahoma, 1950), p. 168; Lewis Cecil Gray, *History of Agriculture in the Southern United States to 1860*, Vol. II (Washington, DC, 1933), p. 853.

[43]See generally Curtis; Wilcox and Smith; and Ensinger.

[44]Ibid.

[45]*USDA Year Book, 1922* (Washington, DC, 1923), p. 278.

[46]Ibid., p. 197; John A. Sims and Leslie E. Johnson, *Animals in the American Economy* (Ames, Ia., 1972), pp. 50–51.

[47]Stevenson Whitcomb Fletcher, *Pennsylvania Agriculture and Country Life, 1640–1840* (Harrisburg, 1950), p. 190; Ulysses Prentiss Hedrick, *A History of Agriculture in the State of New York* (Albany, 1933), p. 376.

[48]Bidwell and Falconer, pp. 436–440.

[49]Ibid.

[50]Bidwell and Falconer, p. 439.

[51]Elmer O. Fippin, *Rural New York* (New York, 1921), p. 236; *USDA Year Book, 1930*, p. 318.

[52]Plumb, p. 497; Thompson, p. 136.

[53]It is unclear, however, whether the first Bedfords ever reached George Washington or not. They reportedly arrived in America through a farmer named Parkinson, who settled in Baltimore, but importation has been dated anywhere from 1760–1800. Report of the US Commissioner of Agriculture, 1872 (Washington, DC, 1872), pp. 298–99; H. C. Dawson, *The Hog Book* (Chicago, 1911), p. 30; Thompson, p. 136; Fletcher, p. 190; B. R. Evans, *The Story of the Durocs: The Truly American Breed of Swine* (Peoria, 1946), p. 11.

[54]*Agricultural Report, 1872*, pp. 298–99; Ulysses Prentice Hedrick, *A History of Agriculture in the State of New York* (Albany, 1933), p. 375; Joseph Ray Davis, *History of the Poland China Breed of Swine*, Vol. I (n. p., 1921).

[55]Plumb, p. 407; Hedrick, p. 375; Thompson, p. 137; Fletcher, p. 190.

[56]*Agricultural Report 1855*, p. 61.

[57]*Agricultural Report, 1855*, p. 61; *Agricultural Report, 1872*, pp. 298–99.

[58]Thompson, p. 136; Towne and Wentworth, p. 168; Davis, pp. 1–2; Dawson, p. 37; Lewis Cecil Gray, *History of Agriculture in the Southern United States to 1860, Vol II* (Washington, DC, 1933), p. 853; Charles William Burkett, *History of Ohio Agriculture* (Concord, New Hampshire, 1900), p. 100. Davis suggests that 1846 was the date as the end of cross–breeding other varieties to produce the Poland China. If it is correct that the Byfield did not survive this development, we should date its extinction sometime after 1850.

[59]Thompson, p. 137; Burkett, p. 142; Hilton M. Briggs and Dinius M. Briggs, *Modern Breeds of Livestock* (New York, 1980), p. 379.

[60]Gray, p. 853; *Agricultural Report, 1853*, Part II, pp. 51–58; *Agricultural Report, 1854*, p. 57; *Agricultural Report, 1855*, p. 61; *Agricultural Report, 1863*, pp. 200–01.

[61]*Agricultural Report, 1863*, p. 201.

[62]Refer to note 58; see also *Agricultural Report, 1867*, p. 310 on the breed's great popularity in Iowa. The animal came highly recommended in at least one 1858 farm manual. Charles L. Flint, *Milch Cows and Dairy Farming* (New York, 1858), p. 362.

[63]*Agricultural Report, 1853*, Pt. II, pp. 52–53.

[64]Vaughan, p. 365.

[65]Dawson, p. 37.

[66]Burkett, pp. 143–44.

[67]Davis, p. 1; Towne and Wentworth, pp. 174–75; *Agricultural Report, 1872*, pp. 426–28.

[68]Evans, pp. 15–17; Towne and Wentworth, pp. 170–171; Hilton M. Briggs and Dinius M. Briggs, *Modern Breeds of Livestock* (New York, 1980), pp. 355–56.

[69]Evans, p. 17; Briggs and Briggs, pp. 355–358.

[70]American Essex Association, *Records of Improved Essex Swine* (New Augusta, Ill., 1890), Vol. I; Ida M. Millen, *The Natural History of the Pig* (New York, 1852), p. 49.

[71]Flint, pp. 362–63.

[72]Plumb, p. 777.

[73]Cheshire Swine Breeder's Association, *Cheshire Herd Book* (Oneida and Chittenango, New York, 1889–1914), Vol. I, pp. 15–16.

[74]Wilcox and Smith, pp. 506–507; Cheshire Swine Breeders Association, Vol. I, pp. 21–23.

[75]Ibid.; Fippin, p. 238.

[76]Cheshire Swine Breeders' Association, Vol. VI.

[77]*USDA Year Book, 1920*, p. 755.

[78]Vaughan, p. 365.

[79]Plumb, pp. 518–19.

[80]Curtis, pp. 310–13.

[81]Ibid.

[82]Vaughan, p. 365.

[83]*USDA Year Book, 1920*, p. 755.

Extinction of Horse Breeds in the United States

Carolyn J. Christman
The American Livestock Breeds Conservancy, Pittsboro, NC

The record of horse extinctions in the United States is crowded with breeds that were imported but later lost as distinct populations. The Friesian, for example, was imported from the Netherlands into New Amsterdam (New York) during the eighteenth century and then probably absorbed by the Morgan. The French Coach Horse, the German Coach Horse (including the Hanoverian, Oldenburg, and Trakehner), and the French Draft Horse all had breed associations and registries operating in 1900 but later disappeared. Other breeds, such as the Dartmoor and the Exmoor, were imported in smaller numbers and with little historical record.

Four breeds are of particular interest in describing the history of horse extinctions in the United States: the Narragansett Pacer, the Cleveland Bay, the Conestoga, and Canadian.

The Narragansett Pacer

The most famous American horse breed to become extinct is the Narragansett Pacer. The story of the Narragansett is also the story of the earliest horse industry in Colonial America. Horses came to the eastern American colonies beginning in the 1630s with Dutch imports to New Amsterdam. Imports from England began in the 1640s. Among the breeds imported from England were the Scottish Galloway and the Irish Hobby. Both of these breeds were considered "amblers," as they moved with a smooth gait (called an amble), instead of a trot, making them especially comfortable to ride.

New England was the chief recipient of imports, and the early center of horse activity was the colony of Rhode Island, settled in 1636 and chartered in 1647. It was here that ambler stock, perhaps with the addition of Spanish jennet (a gaited Spanish breed), was developed into an American breed called the Narragansett Pacer. The Pacer, acclaimed for its easy ride, was well known by the mid-seventeenth century. (The "pace" of the Narragansett was unlike the "pace" of the modern Standardbred. The Narragansett moved with a comfortable four beat pace, while the Standardbred's pace, a two beat gait, oscillates the horse's back from side to side, making for an uncomfortable ride.)

The Narragansett Pacer was developed at the same time that a thriving horse trade arose with the West Indies. The breed was exported in large numbers to be used as a riding horse in sugar plantations. The Narragansett Pacer was an integral part of this early trade relationship; New England sent food, lumber, fish, livestock, and horses to the Indies and in return imported sugar, molasses, rum, dyestuffs, and hard currency with which to buy English goods.

The lucrative export trade, plus the use of imported English forage grasses, led to the rapid expansion of the New England horse industry during the eighteenth century. By the late eighteenth century, however, changes were afoot that would directly affect the Narragansett Pacer.

The Revolutionary War interrupted trade with the West Indies, which only briefly resumed afterwards. In New England, a growing network of roads allowed the expanded use of horse drawn vehicles for transportation, which favored the selection of breeds which could trot fast over long distances — breeds such as the Morgan, Canadian, and Standardbred. The Narragansett Pacer, because it ambled instead of trotting, was deemed unsuitable for harness use.

In the mid-Atlantic states of Pennsylvania, New York, Maryland, and Virginia, the Pacer was gradually displaced by the English Thoroughbred. Thoroughbreds had been imported beginning around 1700, and by about 1800 the breed was dominant as a race horse and as an improver of other stocks. The Thoroughbred had great impact on the development of the Standardbred, the Saddlebred, the Morgan, and the Colonial Quarter Horse. It was larger, faster, and considered more beautiful than the Narragansett Pacer.

A market in the South and on the frontier for smooth riding horses did remain, and the Narragansett Pacer likely found its way west. In fact, it may have been a link between the gaited horses of colonial times and the gaited breeds developed in Kentucky and Tennessee in the 1800s. By and large, however, the era of the Narragansett Pacer was over by 1800 and the breed was lost shortly afterwards.

The Conestoga Horse

A second horse breed which became extinct early in American history was the Conestoga horse. The Conestoga was a draft breed developed for farm work in the Lancaster County area of Pennsylvania during the late eighteenth century. The horse became best known for its use with the Conestoga wagon transportation system, which carried freight from the eastern seaboard to the Ohio River and later moved wagon trains west. Both horse breed and wagon were named after the Conestoga River.

Though the history of the Conestoga was never written, there is speculation that it originated from the cross of Flemish horses from New York and English stock from Virginia. It was a long-limbed, large breed, 17 hands high and weighing 1,400–1,600 pounds. It was common for three teams to pull wagons of 60 feet or more, and the horses did increase in size over time (to perhaps 1,800 pounds) to accommodate heavier wagons. The Conestoga was dark in color with a well-arched crest and docile disposition. It had clean legs with no extra hair (or "feather"), perceived as a nuisance for hauling on muddy roads or in the fields.

The Conestoga horse was considered a valuable part of the Conestoga transportation system. The horses were unusually well kept for the times, and a price of $1,000 per team was not unusual. Yet during the second half of the nineteenth century, the Conestoga fell into decline for two reasons. Attention was turned to imported draft horse breeds, particularly the Percheron, which became the dominant draft horse breed of the nineteenth century. It was the Percheron Horse which was used to work in the fields of the larger farms of the Midwest. In addition, the Conestoga system of transportation itself was replaced by a network of railroads and canals, leaving the breed without its historic job. The Conestoga was likely extinct by 1900.

The Cleveland Bay and the Canadian

The Cleveland Bay also became extinct in the United States, though it did survive elsewhere. The Cleveland was imported from England to the United States beginning in 1819, with a big increase during the 1880s. A breed association was formed in 1885 and it registered 1,000 horses by 1905. Though not relatively numerous, the breed was well known. Buffalo Bill raised Cleveland Bays on his North Platte, Nebraska ranch and drove a hitch of eight Cleveland stallions. By the turn of the century, however, the Cleveland Bay was almost extinct, absorbed into other breeds. It was reimported from England beginning in the 1930s but remains rare in North America and globally.

The Canadian horse was developed from French horses sent to New France by King Louis XIV between 1647 and 1670. Through necessity and selection, the Canadian (or "French Canadian") became a utility horse extraordinaire. It was a fast trotter, hard working draft animal, and stylish saddle horse. Canadian horses were imported into the United States during the eighteenth and nineteenth centuries. Canadian stallions were widely used to improve local stocks and in the development of new breeds; in New England, they made significant genetic contributions to both the Morgan and the Standardbred. In Kentucky, the Canadian stallion Pilot was one of the foundation sires of the American Saddlebred.

However, the lucrative United States market for Canadian horses was a threat to the very survival of the breed in Canada. The horses sent to the United States were not kept as a separate breed, and there was no breed association or registry. In addition, thousands of Canadian horses were killed in the United States Civil War and in the Boer War in Africa. Efforts began in Canada in 1885 to salvage what was left of the Canadian horse and eventually resulted in the breed's conservation. This was essential, as the Canadian was extinct in the United States by this time.

It is common for horse breeds to be lost through absorption into another breed or breeds. If this happens, as it did with the Canadian horse in the United States, the genetics are *used*, often to great benefit, but the breed as a genetic unit is no longer distinguishable and can be considered extinct.

Bibliography

Robert Leslie Jones, "The Old French Canadian Horse: Its History in Canada and the United States," *The Canadian Historical Review* 28:2, 1947.

George Shumway, Edward Durell, and Howard C. Frey, *Conestoga Wagon: 1750–1850*, n. p., n. d.

John Strohm and Herbert H. Beck, "The Conestoga Horse," *Papers of the Lancaster County Historical Society*, 44 (1940).

Kenneth A. Telford, *The Origins of the Modern Morgan: A Study in Contrasts.* (Randolph, Vermont,1988), privately printed by the author.

The author acknowleges the assistance of the Library of the International Museum of the Horse, The Kentucky Horse Park, Lexington, Kentucky, for this research.

Goat Breeds Believed Extinct In North America

Robert L. Johnson
International Dairy Goat Registry, Inc., Rossville, GA

At what point or date the first member of the genus *Capra* set foot on North American soil remains unknown. Since there are no goats native to the Americas, the 15th or 16th century would have seen the first arrivals of Spanish goats. (If the Vikings brought any goats with them, which is quite possible, they did not survive.)

Goats of various types and breeds were brought to the Americas for three centuries with sailors and settlers, and while little is known about the specifics of these arrivals, they doubtless were dominated by the dairy and meat types most useful to travelers and pioneers. Most importations of goats since the mid-19th century are known and documented, beginning with the Angora.

On May 31, 1905, the first American registry of dairy goats was founded, the American Milch Goat Record Association (AMGRA). This organization thrives today as the American Dairy Goat Association (ADGA), the largest American goat registry. The AMGRA published its first herdbook in 1914, stating in the preface that all goats registered as pure breeds should trace their ancestry directly back to importations from Europe, though lamenting that this was not always possible.

AMGRA's early herdbooks reveal the existence of a variety of goat breeds. Though the Toggenburg and Saanen breeds were clearly most popular, there were also a large number of goats among the first 124 registered listed as "breed unknown" or "not given."

The herdbooks also include some unusual breeds:

(1) *Indian.* This could refer to a Nubian or a variant that the breeder wished to distinguish.

(2) *Calcutta Llama.* This is the most curious listing of all, for no other references to this breed are known to the author, despite considerable research in books of the same era. One can surmise that this might also refer to a Nubian variant. It seems unlikely that a dairy goat organization would have been persuaded to register a true llama.

(3) *Spanish Maltese.* Goats from the island of Malta are reported to have reached the Southwest by the 1940s, a claim somewhat verified by the USDA's 1946 bulletin #920 on milk goats. It is likely that other Spanish breeds may have reached the United States from Mexico over the years, but were amalgamated into the so-called Spanish meat goats of today.

(4) *Schwartzenberg-Guggisberger.* The pioneering importations of Fred Stucker of Liberty, New York, had much influence on American goatkeeping. "Stucker" is a proud name in the distant background of

many Saanens. The Schwartzenberg-Guggisberger, which has been called a "white Toggenburg," was a popular dairy breed in Germany and Switzerland, though their status today is unknown.

(5) *Murcien.* This Spanish breed first appeared in AMGRA's registry as imported February 13, 1922. The Murcien, Murciene, or Royal Murciana is an old Spanish dairy breed, usually a deep mahogany color but occasionally solid black. Murciens had undoubtedly been brought in on other occasions as early as the 17th century. Will TeWalt, in *Improved Milk Goats* (1944), stated that the Murciene was "introduced several years back from Spain." The International Dairy Goat Record Association, established in 1929 in Nebraska, included Royal Murciana goats in the five breeds it registered, and Frank Coutant's *ABC of Goat Dairying* briefly mentioned Murcianas. Murciens were crossed on other Spanish breeds then native to the Southwest and their identity was lost. They remain an important dairy breed in Spain.

(6) *Norska.* A very old and popular Norwegian breed which apparently was imported on one or possibly two occasions, the first in October, 1926, when five does and one buck were brought in from Oslo by Cris Goplin. The breed is described in volumes II (1943) and III (1944) of Carl W. Romer's annual *American Dairy Goat Year Book.* Two types were recognized: the Nord Torpa type, which is predominately white, black, and gray; and the Telemark type, predominately white, and a dominant breed in Norway today. Despite enthusiastic support and promotion of the breed, no subsequent references to it have surfaced.

(7) *Rock Alpine.* The noted breeder Mary Rock devoted much of her life to creating the Rock Alpine from French and Swiss Alpine import stock, and AMGRA recognized it as a separate breed by 1922. Coutant's book claimed that all Rock Alpines must trace to the 1904 Canadian importation of Alpines, specifically to a doe "Molly Crepin I." Rock Alpines found numerous followers and the breed was maintained for several decades. The Rock Alpine flourished until the 1960s and was then lost through outbreeding with French Alpines. ADGA no longer recognizes it as a separate breed.

These seven breeds are extinct in the United States today. From time to time one encounters other breed names, the most common being Swiss Alpine, which was used through the 1960s for the dairy breed known today as the Oberhasli.

The recorded history of goats and goat breeds in the United States is far more limited than that available for other species. It is often not clear if breed names refer to true breeds, local strains, or simply the geographical location of the population. For example, some brush goats from the Appalachian Mountains in north Georgia were known as "Rome" goats (there is a Rome, Georgia; could there have been a goat market there for a time?). Other Appalachian native or brush goats have been advertised as "Tennessee Mountain" goats. Myotonic goats are called Wooden Leg, Nervous, Stiff-Leg, Fainting, Fall-Down, and Tennessee.

Having no native goats, America has depended on importations for the ancestors of the millions of goats extant here today. Much credit is due the many breeders who labored patiently to improve the stock they had available over the past decades. It is to be regretted that some breeds have been lost to extinction.

Appendix II

The North American Feral Livestock Census

Carolyn J. Christman and D. Phillip Sponenberg
The American Livestock Breeds Conservancy, Pittsboro, NC

Feral animals are those which have reversed the course of domestication to become free living once again. They live without human interference, shaped directly by natural selection. Dramatic physical and behavioral changes can occur as animals become feral. Long term adaptations, especially to challenging or unusual environments, can result in unique genetic characteristics.

In spite of the possibility that some strains are genetically unique, feral animals in general are not well understood, do not attract much scientific interest, and remain nearly invisible to those concerned about livestock breeding. It is only when feral animals compete, and particularly when they outcompete, managed domestic animals or wild species that they become visible, and then almost always as environmental problems. Too often, feral populations are destroyed before being studied.

Geographer Tom L. McKnight of the University of California at Los Angeles wrote the initial discourse on feral livestock with his 1964 monograph *Feral Livestock in Anglo-America*.[1] McKnight's census included feral burros, cattle, cats, dogs, goats, horses, pigs, and sheep of North America, with listings of populations by species and state or province. The report provided insightful discussions of each species, including potential to become feral, ability to survive in the feral state, locations of feral populations, patterns of life, problems caused, and prospects for the future.

McKnight's work, although now almost thirty years old, remains the single most important description of feral livestock. Subsequent studies of feral animals have largely focused on single populations, detailing interactions with wildlife, plant, and physical habitat. Much of the current research on feral animals is contract work done to promote specific land-use policies, usually the removal of feral populations. No other continent-wide survey has considered the overall geography of feral stocks, their status, significance, and prospects.

One obstacle in feral research is the actual definition of "feral" itself. Generally, feral animals are considered to be any domestic animals now free living, regardless of the amount of time in the wild. McKnight's criteria were similarly broad:

"a feral animal is one that was once domesticated, or with domesticated ancestors, but now lives as a wild creature. It is not under the effective ownership of humans, and does not receive protection, care, or food as a deliberate gift from man. In this study, then, are considered animals that definitely are feral, as well as some that are more truly 'loose' than feral"[1].

The ALBC Feral Livestock Census

Methods

The first step of the ALBC census was to document, if possible, the status of all of the populations described by McKnight in 1964. The second step was to determine which stocks were likely to be genetically significant. Most feral populations have experienced periodic additions of animals of varying genetic backgrounds and are therefore genetic mixtures. By contrast, isolated, well defined populations, particularly those which have adapted to harsh environments, are more likely to be of genetic importance.

The census included burros, cattle, horses, sheep, and goats in the United States and in Canada, although resources were depleted before the completion of the western goat populations. The John Mayer and I. Lehr Brisbin book *Wild Pigs in the United States: Their History, Comparative Morphology, and Current Status* (University of Georgia Press, 1991) serves as an excellent update of the feral hog populations in the United States, so this effort was not duplicated for the ALBC feral census.

Research was initiated in 1987–1988, with mail questionnaires sent to 400 animal scientists, conservation professionals, and managers of state and federal lands. Telephone followup interviews were conducted in 1989–1990 and eventually accounted for most of the data collected. Both mail and telephone questionnaires requested specific information (e.g., number of animals, characteristics, history, introductions, exact geographical location) about each feral population reported by McKnight.

Results

Results are given by species. For each species, the data given by McKnight are compared with the data gathered by ALBC. Where specific sources were consulted, they are coded and listed at the end of the report. Data published by the Bureau of Land Management were the basis for most of the information on burros and horses.

Burros

Feral burros and horses in the United States, unlike other feral livestock species, are protected on public lands by the 1971 Wild Horse and Burro Protection Act. Burros (and horses) are managed by the

Bureau of Land Management (BLM) of the United States Department of the Interior. The BLM includes feral burro range as one of the several uses of federal lands (including permitted cattle grazing) it must balance. The agency is mandated to regulate numbers of burros and their locations, but is not permitted to eradicate feral burros; in fact, it is illegal to kill burros on the public lands described in the 1971 law. Animals considered "excess" may, however, be removed and sold to the public. United States national parks, national wildlife refuges, and national monuments are not covered by federal statutes and may eradicate burros. There are no feral burros known in Canada.

Federal protection in 1971 may have allowed growth in population of burros on public lands beyond the 13,000 described by McKnight in 1964. However, the implementation of BLM land management policies has meant a shrinking of range allotted for burros, as well as an eventual decrease in numbers. The BLM has removed for adoption over 10,000 burros since 1971, which is more than the approximately 5,000 burros that now run free on the continent. The agency is committed to further reductions of burro populations in the areas of greatest population densities — the lower Colorado River and the California Desert Area. It may be that BLM burro management policies, done without fanfare, will do what harsh desert conditions and a bare existence cannot do: reduce numbers and ranges so drastically that feral burros will be left in only a few isolated areas of North America.

Burros are unquestionably one of the hardiest of all feral species. Little research has been done to explore possible genetic differences between wild burros and domestic donkeys. Such documentation might serve to justify maintenance of feral burro herds on public lands and registration of them as a separate breed within the donkey registries.

---

[1]T. L. McKnight, "Feral Livestock in Anglo-America", *University of California Publications in Geography* 16, 1964.

Table II.1
Areas with Populations of Feral Burros, by State, 1964 and 1987

1964[1] Area (population)	1987 Area (population)	Management Activity	BLM Target Population
	———— Arizona ————		
State Total (2,000–4,000)	State Total (3,625)	5,890 captured 1977–1986; 3,282 placed for adoption	835
Black/Galiuro Mountains near Tucson (a few)	Galiuro Mountains (?)	?	
Black Mountains (several hundred)	Black Mountain – BLM (1,045) Lake Mead – BLM (1,200–1,500)	reduction removal	400 0
Bill Williams River (several dozen)	Havasu – BLM (121)	?	170
Grand Canyon NP (several hundred)	Grand Canyon NP (0)	removed in 1980–1981	0
Kofa NWR and Castle Dome (several dozen)	Cibola – BLM (42) Trigo – BLM (372) Imperial NWR (400)	removal reduction removal	0 165 0
Mohawk/Cabeza Prieta (some)	Cabeza Prieta – BLM (0)	removed	0
Organ Pipe NM (a few)	Organ Pipe NM (0)	total pop. (106) was removed in 1976	0
Wickenberg (a few)	?	?	
?	Big Sandy – BLM	removal of 258 since 1983	
	———— California ————		
State Total (2,500–5,000)	State Total (2,765)		700
Arawatz Mountains (a few)	?		
Chemehuevi Range, Whipple Mountains (several dozen)	Chemehuevi – BLM (259)	reduction	150
Clark Mountain (a few)	Clark Mountain – BLM (67)	109 removed	44
Coso, Argus Mountains (3,000–4,000)	China Lake Naval Reserve (1,300)	8,000 removed	0
Death Valley (West)	Death Valley NM (2,000–3,000) in 1983	6,000 removed	0
Imperial Co. (a few)	Chocolate Mountains, Mules BLM (255)	reduction/fencing	22
Merced River Valley (between Bagby and Hornitos) (a few)	?		

150

Table II.1 (continued)

Panamint Mountains	Panamints – BLM (100)	reduction	0
Saline Valley, N Death Valley (800–1,200)	Saline Valley, N Death Valley (115)	?	357
San Bernardino Co. (500–2,000)	Mohave Desert ? (298)	?	130
San Bernardino Mountains, Barton Flats (a few)	?		
San Bernardino Mountains, North Slope (a few)	?		
South Sierra Nevadas, Eastern Side (a few)	?		
Smoke Creek, near Ravendale (a few)	?		
?	Granite/Providence Mountains	279 removed in 1982, 1985	?

——————— Colorado ———————

State Total (50–100)	State Total (0)		700
Fort Garland area of San Luis Valley (a few)	?		

——————— Idaho ———————

State Total (50–100)	State Total (0)		700
Owyhee Canyon in the SW corner of Idaho (a few)	?		

——————— Nevada ———————

State Total (700–1,500)	State Total (1,202)		0
Charles Sheldon Antelope Range, Virgin Valley (a few)	Charles Sheldon (0)		0
Mtn Ranges near Colorado River, Lake Mead (several hundred)	Lake Mead NWR (1,200–1,500)	reductions	0
Piper Peak area, SW of Goldfield (a few)	Piper Peak (?)	?	0
Smoke Creek Desert, Pyramid Lake	Susanville	?	
Wassuk Range (a few)	?		

——————— New Mexico ———————

State Total (500–900)	State Total (14?)		0?
Bandelier NM (a few dozen)	Bandelier NM (6–8)	146 removed since 1979	0

151

Table II.1 (continued)

Copper Canyon (a few)	?		
Luera and Elk Mtns (a few)	?		
Mesa Prieta (a few)	?		
Tularosa Basin (a few)	?		

——————— Oregon ———————

State Total (25)	State Total (25)		

——————— South Dakota ———————

State Total (?)	State Total (25)		
?	Custer State Park	4–8 live-trapped each year	25

——————— Texas ———————

State Total (25–50)	State Total (0)		
Big Bend NP (a few)	Big Bend NP 0	removal	0

——————— Utah ———————

State Total (50–150)	State Total (34)		
Area around the confluence of the Colorado and San Juan Rivers (a few)	?		

[1] McKnight, 1964

Cattle

Much of what McKnight wrote about feral cattle in 1964 remains true. Cattle are still both scarce and inconspicuous, found in a very few locations, and occur primarily as temporary and incidental feral populations. McKnight attributes this pattern in part to the nature of domestic bovines, which are less agile, less skittish, and less individualistic than equines and so have less inherent proclivity to become feral. Also, once they are feral, cattle are easier to round up and more relentlessly pursued as table fare.

Cattle become feral when landscape and management permit strays from range herds to wander away and form bands. Bands of cattle can remain in areas too isolated to be easily worked for a few years or even a few generations, and cattle born in the wild are apt to become very wild indeed. However, the number of feral cattle is now even more limited than twenty-five years ago. Only a few of the populations described from 1964 remain. Indeed, the majority of the populations described by McKnight were likely range cattle that were managed, albeit loosely, through the turning out of bulls and subsequent harvest of calves. Feral herds are generally transitory.

Conditions for ranging cattle have changed in the past twenty-five years. Range laws have been imposed in the lower South to provide for more intense use of land for timbering, hunting, and development. In the West, the competition for federal land use is heated. Despite the long-held primacy of permitted cattle grazing, the costs of this special interest are being raised by those who manage federal refuges, forests, and parks. Increased pressure by competing interests may gradually limit the rights of ranchers to use public lands as freely as they once did, and limitations on cattle ranging in turn limit the opportunities for cattle to become feral.

Table II.2
Areas with Populations of Feral Cattle, by State, 1964 and 1990

1964[1] Area	1990 Current population (source)
——————— Alabama ———————	
River bottoms of Clark and Washington counties in SW Alabama, near Mobile	Probably not present. (AK3, AK5, AK6, AK7)

Note: Extensively managed "Pineywoods" cattle have been widely known in the Deep South for centuries. Stock laws enacted in the last twenty-five years, however, now limit the ranging of cattle. It is only in the most remote areas that small bands may still survive, and even there it's likely they have been crossed with domestic Brahman bulls.

——————— Alaska ———————	
Shumagin Islands	Shumangin, including Simeonoff Island, not present, removed 1984–1985. (AK6, AK7, AK8)
Chirikoff Island	Still present – about 500 head of extensively managed range cattle, with BLM permits (AK7, AK8) Sinak Island has 600–700 range cattle, owned by Cane Cove Native Corporation but only minimally managed. Cattle have been on the island since the 1920s; maybe this same herd, maybe not. (AK8)

Note: Cattle have been raised on the Aleutians since late in the 1800s. Highland cattle predominated initially, though Hereford, Angus, and other commercial breeds have also been introduced. There has been culling of bulls and selection against horned animals. The habitat is very harsh, and some of these populations are marginal in the winter, suffering die-offs during the winters and requiring replacements in the spring.

153

Table II.2 (continued)

──────── **Arizona** ────────

Arizona Strip	Probably not present, in fact, transitory groups of cattle are historic to the area rather than stable feral herds. (AZ17, UT9)
Fort Apache, San Carlos Indian Reservation	Not feral, there used to be cattle ranged here, but always owmed and managed. Cattle are no longer ranged here (UT7)
Graham Mountains	Not present. Only cattle known in the past were owned and range managed. (AZ18)
Kofa Game Range	Not present. Residual animals were rounded up in the 1960s. (AZ15)
Navajo Indian Reservation	Not present; probably never a feral population. (UT7)
Superstition Mountains	Not present. A band of steers present in the area during the mid-1960s, but was rounded up and removed. (AZ16)

──────── **California** ────────

Bontgunwale Canyon, Tehama Co.	Not present. This area has been open range for cattle ranching, but the winter snow is too deep to allow for cattle year around.(CA19)
Death Valley NM Hunter Mount, Grapevine Range	Not present. (CA17)
Granite & Santa Rosa Mountains, Riverside Co.	Maybe a few here and there. Anza Borrego State Park has removed 120 unbranded cattle from the park over the past 18 years. There may be a few more in the eastern part of the county, though it is inhospitable range.(CA18, CA22)
Santa Catalina Island	Not present. Most of the cattle were removed by the late 1950s, and the rest since then. These cattle were remnants of the island's historic ranching operations. (CA16)

──────── **Florida** ────────

"Various places along the west coast, in marsh and swamp land and along river bottoms, though not in large numbers."	Probably not present. (FL2)

Note: Feral cattle used to occur on lands now being used more intensively for timbering and for hunting. Cattle competed with deer and so have been removed from some areas. In other places, they have been absorbed into the general population, diluted by the release of commercial bulls. It is not likely that any genetically unique feral stocks remain in Florida.

──────── **Georgia** ────────

Ft. Stewart Military Reserve	Not present. There have historically been a small number of cattle on the reserve, but all were probably owned. They were removed or hunted between 1955 and 1974. (GA4)

154

Table II.2 (continued)

Okefenokee Swamp   Probably still there, Okefenokee NWR. (GA2)
since the 1870s or earlier

Note: This area was used as range for cattle until the mid-1970s, and many cattle were turned out here. When the area became a refuge, cattle grazing was ended. Cattle found on the refuge may be shot, but there has been no concerted effort to harvest or remove them or to collect those on the fringes of the refuge. There is documentation of regular removal of cattle from the Okefenokee Swamp to replenish domestic herds of "Pineywoods" and "Cracker" cattle.

──────── Hawaii ────────

Mauna Loa on   Two types are present: feral "longhorn" cattle, of which there
Hawaii, the big   are perhaps twenty, and range domestic cattle that have
island   cattle that have wandered away from ranches and are of
     Hereford/Angus type. (HI7)

──────── Louisiana ────────

Generally in river   Probably no true feral herds left, even those in the swamps
bottoms, specifically   likely diluted with Brahma or Zebu. (LA6)
in Ouachita River in
Caldwell Parish, north
central Louisiana

     Wild cattle known in the Atchafalaya Basin, St. Martin's
     Parish, 150–200 head on hunting club lands, there
     since the 1970's. (LA4)
     Wild cattle known in the Atchafalaya Basin, Iberia Parish,
     15–20 head on state lands, since the 1950s. (LA5)

──────── North Carolina ────────

None   Cattle described on Shackleford Banks, a herd of about 100
     that were ranged on the island. They were removed from the
     island in 1986 by the National Park Service when the island
     became part of Cape Lookout National Seashore.

──────── Nevada ────────

East of Pyramid Lake   Not present; no knowledge of a feral population. (NV1)

──────── New Mexico ────────

San Mateo Mountains   Probably not present. There might be a group of five or ten,
     but not for certain. (NM17)

──────── Utah ────────

Book Cliffs   Not present. (UT11)

Colorado River,   Not present. (UT10, UT11)
scattered bands

Note: Occasionally, trespass cattle have been known. One group of 40 range cattle was rounded up five years ago.

Table II.2 (continued)

Green River, scattered bands	Not present. (UT10, UT11)
Henry Mountains	location ?
Monti-La Sal NF, Dark Canyon Plateau	Not present; occasionally there are commercial cattle escapees. (UT12)

——————— **Virginia** ———————

Dismal Swamp	Not present. There were a few owned cattle run in the swamp until removed ten or twelve years ago. (VA3)

[1] McKnight, 1964

Goats

Goats are small in size, hardy in constitution, and adaptable to a wide range of environments and ecosystems. It is quite possible that they are, as McKnight described in 1964, the most widely distributed feral livestock species in North America, ranging from the deep South of the United States into Canada and Alaska.

Goats become feral as a result of escape or abandonment from domestic herds, most often of dairy goats or angoras. They live in small bands, often two dozen or fewer. Most bands are relatively recent in origin and transitory. As one survey respondent remarked, feral goats are only feral as long as no one knows about them, then they are dinner. Mainland populations of feral goats rarely compete with other livestock or wildlife for resources, and so generate relatively less concern among land managers and less interest among academics than do island populations.

It is only on islands lacking predators where feral goats have thrived as large populations over long periods of time. Goats have been so plentiful for centuries on the Hawaiian Islands and on the Channel Islands of California that they were historically used as a game animal. Their large numbers have resulted in dramatic environmental impact, causing their removal from some locations. The physical isolation that makes island flora and fauna so interesting and significant for conservationists has had essentially the same impact on goats, leading to the development of interesting and unique populations. The goats of the Channel Islands in particular are quite significant historically and genetically.

Any census of feral goats is a rough estimate. Most feral goat populations are practically undocumented, not just in their history but even in their basic description. Many populations of goats described by McKnight have not yet been accounted for in the ALBC census, leaving several available for future study. Research on the feral goats of West Virginia was done by Cathy Gorman.

156

Table II.3
Areas with Populations of Feral Goats, by State, 1964 and 1990

1964[1] Area (population)	1990 Current population (source)
————— Alabama —————	
Dallas, Morgan, and Perry Counties in north Alabama, near Decatur (one of the largest eastern populations)	May be some feral goats, but no information about their history or characteristics is available. They are probably still found on timber land, especially where hunting is restricted. (AL9) Doubtful that any feral goats remain. (AL1, AL2)
————— Alaska —————	
Kodiak Island, northern end	Only goats known are domestic milk goats. (AK7)
————— Arizona —————	
Granite, Wash Mountains, Yuma county	Small bands in this general area: Cabeza Prieta NWR – a band of about 50 multi-colored goats was seen crossing the border from Mexico in 10/86; three goats were seen in 2/87. (AZ3) Band of 20–30 Spanish type goats (many were white) from Mexican herds known in the High Tanks Mountains, south of Yuma. There was a stable band, at least from 1967 to 1983 (when respondent's job was patrolling the area). (AZ4)
Eight other populations	Not accounted for.
————— Arkansas —————	
Heavner area of Ouachita NF	Not present in the National Forest. (AR3)
————— California —————	
Santa Catalina Island (several thousand, an important game animal, present for more than 100 years)	Thousands remain, but slated for removal in the next five years. (CA15, CA16, CA21)
San Clemente Island	Population of several thousand reduced by hunting, shooting, and removal in the 1970s and 1980s. A small number of goats, perhaps 100, may remain, but will be killed as found. (CA16) A small domestic population has been established on the mainland.
Santa Cruz Island (a few hundred)	Removed 15–20 years ago. (CA13, CA20)
28 other populations	Not accounted for.

Table II.3 (continued)

──────── **Colorado** ────────

Thirteen other populations	Not accounted for.

──────── **Georgia** ────────

Edgewood Arsenal	location? (GA4)
Lake Lanier Island	Not present in the Lake Lanier Island State Park. (GA3)

──────── **Idaho** ────────

One other population	Not accounted for.

──────── **Kentucky** ────────

Fort Knox	Not aware of any. (KY3)

──────── **Mississippi** ────────

None	A population of road-side goats was described for Claiborne and Jefferson counties. They are domestic goats but roam free most of the time (MS4)

──────── **Missouri** ────────

	A population of eight feral goats on private land is described for Jefferson City river bluffs, present for 15–20 years. (MO2)
One population	Not accounted for.

──────── **Montana** ────────

Five populations	Not accounted for.

──────── **New Mexico** ────────

	A population of twelve goats (trespass Angoras) was discovered in the Martha Skeen Allotment of Broke-Off Mountains in 1985 by the BLM, which promptly removed them as trespass animals. No longer present. (NM5)
	A population of 25 goats was described for the Sacramento Mountains of the Lincoln National Forest. They are believed to be of Spanish type, and may have been present since the 1930s. (NM7)
Six other populations	Not accounted for.

──────── **North Carolina** ────────

	Goats reported for Shackleford Banks, a herd of about 125 which was removed by the National Park Service in 1986 when the island became part of Cape Lookout National Seashore. Goats were descendants of those put out to range by nearby islanders, but nothing is known of their type.

Table II.3 (continued)

Two populations   Not accounted for.

──────── Oregon ────────

Six populations   Not accounted for.

──────── South Carolina ────────

None   Goats described for Botany Bay Island, near Charleston. A small group of goats was introduced to the island in the 1950s by a private individual to graze down interior portions of the maritime forest and wetlands. There were subsequent reintroductions of stock as many goats died due to seasonal fluctuations in food supply. The entire group of 30 goats was removed by the South Carolina Nature Conservancy in 1988. (SC2)

──────── South Dakota ────────

One population   Not accounted for.

──────── Texas ────────

Big Bend NP   Not present. (TX1)

One other population   Not accounted for.

──────── Utah ────────

Colorado River below Moab   Not present. (UT10)

Three other populations   Not accounted for.

──────── Virginia ────────

Assateague Island   Not present. (MD4)

Big Stone Gap, Wise Co.   location?

Chincoteague Island   Not present. (VA4)

Shenandoah National Park   Not present. (VA1)

──────── West Virginia ────────

Black Mountain area near Marlinton   Goats known previously from the head of the Williams River and also the Foreknobs section of the Monongahela River, but no longer present. Probably hunted, captured, or re-domesticated. (WV4, WV8, WV10)

Blake Fork Creek drainage (Parsons)   Not known since the early 1960s. (WV9)

Blue Creek (Kanawa County)   There used to be a well-known feral herd, but it is no longer present. (WV14, WV15)

Great Cacapon Mountain (near Morgan Creek)   Not present, due in part to increased competition from deer. (WV7)

Table II.3 (continued)

Nathaniel Mountain and New River area (Hampshire County)	Not present, due in part to increased competition from deer (WV7) or to hunting. (WV16)
	Population described for Panther Knob (North Fork Mountain, Pendleton County), 20–30 individuals, stable since 1985; these are large, shaggy, white goats. (WV6)
	Population described for the Green-land Gap area of Grant County, all white does with a black buck, present since about 1974. (WV13)

——— **British Columbia** ———

Goats described on the Prairie Hill slope, Saturna Island, one of the outer gulf islands in the Georgia Strait off Vancouver. They are on private land, but the owners of the land do not want them destroyed. There is a population of 75-125 that has been present for 60–100 years. The goats are similar in type to English "crofter goats." They are not protected in any way and are occasionally hunted, though the island is accessible only by boat. (BC3, BC4)

——— **Ontario** ———

Hen Islands in Lake Erie	Not present. The Lake in this area freezes solid in the winter; goats on the island could simply walk to the nearest land in search for food. (ON1)

[1] McKnight, 1964

It is not clear how additional goat populations should be located and evaluated, particularly since to a great extent individual stocks have to be seen to be evaluated as to genetic significance. Based on the very limited information people have about feral goats and the small numbers of animals in each band, efforts to account for the 70 remaining populations listed in McKnight's 1964 survey were discontinued.

Horses

The best known and loved of all feral livestock are wild horses. The feral horse is a symbol of freedom, wildness, and beauty. Tremendously hardy and versatile, wild horses roam from Mexico to Alaska and number well over 20,000. Most of these horses are protected by law. Their management now requires a budget and bureaucracy to cope with the demanding logistics of management and the political fallout management practices sometimes create with animal rights groups, which are organized around wild horse issues as around no other.

The introduction of the horse had a profound impact on the settlement and society of North America. Horses were imported by Spanish explorers and colonists beginning in the 1600s and escapees became feral shortly thereafter. Huge herds of horses roamed the plains by the middle of the eighteenth century and total numbers may have reached several million by the time of the Civil War. As parts of the range were closed, however, herds were pushed from the Great Plains to the Rocky Mountains and westward. Numbers fluctuated, for as long as settlers moved west and farmers and homesteaders abandoned their stock, there were always new horses joining herds.

For most of their history, feral horses were viewed as pests, yet during the Boer War and World War I, the market for horses exploded. Feral herds were rounded up to be sold to dealers and in turn to the military. When machinery replaced animal power after World War II, new markets for wild horses were developed, chiefly the use of horses for pet food and for export of horse meat to Europe. Increased federal regulation of the range encouraged the removal of unclaimed, loose stock.

During the 1940s and 1950s, horse roundups were common, and airplanes and helicopters were used to capture or kill thousands of animals. Public concerns about the mustangs and the methods of capture increased during the 1950s. During the 1960s, federal laws were passed to forbid mustanging with motorized equipment, and the "Wild Free-roaming Horse and Burro Act" of 1971 gave federal protection to horses and burros on designated public lands. With some notable exceptions, wild horses on public lands could no longer be killed, either by individuals or by the government. The law established use by wild horse herds as one of multiple uses to be considered in federal land use planning.

Horse numbers grew dramatically as a result of federal protection and management by the Bureau of Land Management (BLM). By 1980, there were an estimated 50,000 wild horses on BLM lands in the United States — quite an increase over McKnight's 1964 estimate of between 18,000 and 34,000. During the 1980s, the BLM sought to reduce the numbers of horses on the range, though their options for dealing with "excess" stocks were limited chiefly to the adopt-a-horse program, which resettled 80,000 wild mustangs.

Almost all feral horses in the United States are under BLM jurisdiction in ten western states and 270 herd areas. Therefore, BLM data are nearly complete feral horse data. Since BLM herd management areas do not match the geographical areas described by McKnight, however, matching populations is very difficult. Instead, we have provided state totals for 1964 and 1988 where the BLM manages horses. Additional information is given for eastern and Canadian horses, which are not under BLM jurisdiction.

Table II.4
Populations of Feral Horses Managed by the Bureau of Land Management

State	1964[1]	1980	1988
Arizona	25–50	125	204
California	800–1,800	2,897	1,755
Colorado	500–1,500	1,229	569
Idaho	500–2,500	935	449
Montana	500–800	232	128
Nevada	5,000–7,000	31,260	27,015
New Mexico	3,000–5,000	76	70
North Dakota	0–250	0	
Oregon	2,000–4,000	3,458	2,549
Utah	1,200–2,500	1,714	1,319
Washington	500–2,000	0	0
Wyoming	300–800	10,448	3,764

[1] McKnight, 1964

Table II.5
Populations of Feral Horses in Canada and the Eastern United States

1964[1] Area (population)	1990 Current population (source)
	——— Georgia ———
Big Cumberland, Little Cumberland, Little St. Simon's Islands off of the coast of GA, but under loose ownership pattern, regularly rounded up so not really feral (400–500)	Horses are still present on Big Cumberland (100–200), most likely there since the 1920s or 1930s. They are under study and may be removed as Cumberland is now a National Seashore. (GA2, GA3, GA4)
	——— Louisiana ———
None	A herd of 40–50 horses is described for St. Martin's Parish. They are of no particular breed and have been there for 15–20 years. (LA3)

Table II.5 (continued)

———— Maryland ————

None	Assateague Island, shared by Maryland and Virginia, has a herd of wild ponies. Horses have been known on the island for 250 years, but it is not known if herds have been there continuously. Introductions of stock have been made regularly, though relatively few survive. Herds of the two states have been separated since 1965. The Maryland herd, owned by the National Park Service, has been unmanaged since 1965 and there have been no outside introductions. (MD1, MD2, MD3)

———— North Carolina ————

Noted ponies on several Outer Banks islands, but felt they were under an ownership pattern and subject to roundups, so not considered feral	Horses are located in three herds: Currituck/Corolla (150), some owned, some wild; Ocracoke (20), owned by the National Park Service, which fences and feeds them; and Shackleford Banks (100). A few (25?) may still be found on Carrot Island near Beaufort. (NC1, NC2, NC3, NC4)

Note: These "Banker" ponies are of great local interest, pride, and mythology. While ponies have been known on the islands of the Outer Banks since the time of the Spanish, the link between the historical animals and modern ones is unclear. It is unlikely that the modern herds are direct descendants of Spanish stocks; more likely that they come from horses ranged on the islands earlier this century.

———— Virginia ————

Noted ponies on Chinco-teague Island but felt they were under an ownership pattern marked by annual roundups	Ponies have been on Chincoteague and Assateague for centuries, although the exact link with historic Spanish horses is unclear. Ponies are now found only on Assateague. The Virginia herd is owned by the town of Chincoteague, managed with an annual roundup, public sale, and medical care as required by law for sales to occur. Many introductions to the herd have been made. (MD3, VA2)

———— Alberta ————

Rocky Mountain foothills area, bewteen Highwood and Athabaska Rivers, with a few elsewhere of the herds (1,500–2,000)	Horses are present, maybe 500 (AB2), maybe fewer (AB3); the genetic makeup is unknown.

———— British Columbia ————

Thompson, Upper Fraser River drainages (1,000–2,000)	Certainly fewer and more scattered than in 1964, but little information is available. (BC2)

———— Nova Scotia ————

Sable Island, 100 miles east of the Nova Scotia mainland (200–300)	Still present and protected by Canadian law (350) (NS1). This is a unique strain of old Coldblood type and the only North American feral horse not of Spanish origin.

[1] McKnight, 1964

Sheep

McKnight describes sheep as the livestock species least equipped to become feral and consequently the least widespread of feral livestock. Sheep are susceptible to inclement weather and serve as ready prey for many carnivores. In addition, the flocking behavior desirable in domestic sheep can be counterproductive for sheep in the wild, particularly in times or areas of scant forage. In 1964, feral sheep were found in only six states and appeared in large numbers in only two settings (Hawaii and California's Channel Islands), where climates are mild and predators practically nonexistent. McKnight commented that sheep are the easiest of the feral livestock to control, which he considered fortunate since he also judged them the most likely to do environmental damage. He speculated that most feral sheep would likely be eliminated or replaced by game sheep in the future.

McKnight's analysis holds true twenty-five years later. There has been widespread growth in the development of private hunting ranches, many of which use Mouflons and other horned sheep as game animals. These sheep will generally outcompete (or occasionally crossbreed with) feral sheep, which are not themselves considered a game animal.

Feral sheep have thrived only on islands, and there they have developed and retained unique genetic traits. The Santa Cruz Island sheep, the subject of an ALBC conservation program since 1988, are genetically significant and make a strong case for careful evaluation of any feral sheep stocks prior to eradication.

Table II.6
Areas with Populations of Feral Sheep, by State, 1964 and 1990

1964[1] Area (population)	1990 Current population (source)
———————— Alabama ————————	
Hill country of Morgan County (a few)	Not present. (AL1, AL8, AL10)

Note: Sheep, and extensive management of sheep, were not nearly as common as cattle in the Deep South. People have heard of feral sheep, but not recently.

| ———————— California ———————— | |
| Santa Cruz Island (moderate numbers) | Population of 3,000 in 1986–1987 (CA23), but now there is only a small remnant population on the island and a small managed population on the mainland. Most of the sheep were removed by The Nature Conservancy by 1987–1988 in order to protect and restore plant life of the island. ALBC has established a conservation program on the mainland for *ex situ* conservation of the breed. |

Table II.6 (continued)

San Miguel Island   Not present. (CA12, CA16, CA20)
(moderate numbers
from the 1940s)

Note: Not much is known about these sheep. They were likely escapees when island ranches closed in the 1940s. Many sheep were gathered then; the rest have been removed by the National Park Service.

———————— **Colorado** ————————

Picnic flats area of   Not present; probably were escapees from Ute flocks. (CO6)
southern Ute Indian
Reservation in south-
western Colorado
(a small number, but
an established band)

———————— **Hawaii** ————————

Island of Hawaii   Still present, numbering between 500 and 2,000 (HI4). Most
(especially Mauna   are Mouflon, not domestic sheep. (HI7)
Kea, Mauna Loa,
Mount Hualalai)

Note: Feral sheep are slated for eradication from Mauna Kea and other public lands. Mouflon cross animals predominate due to local interest in hunting sheep. Feral domestics are quite rare if still present at all.

———————— **North Carolina** ————————

None   Sheep described for Shackleford Banks, perhaps from the
1800s; a flock of 125 was removed by the National Park
Service in 1986. The sheep were communally owned and
periodically rounded up to raise money for a local fire
department. Specific information about the sheep is
unavailable.

———————— **Oregon** ————————

Jefferson County, Trout   Still present. (OR5, OR11)
and Hay Creek drainages
(a small number but an
established feral band)

Note: There is a growing population of horned game sheep in Oregon, including Barbados, Barbary, and Mouflon. These animals have been introduced by private game ranches but now also run on public lands. A few domestic sheep are mixed in, but it is unlikely there is still a distinct band of domestic sheep. The state has planned reintroductions of bighorn sheep, which will require removal of the game sheep. There is already one court case pending on this issue.

———————— **Utah** ————————

Split Mountain Gorge in   Probably not present; sheep have not been known in the Split
northeastern Utah (a small   Mountain Gorge area of Dinosaur National Monument for at
number but an established   least 17 years. (UT8)
feral band)

---

[1] McKnight, 1964

165

Genetic Evaluation of Feral Populations

The goal of the North American Feral Livestock Census was to locate feral populations that are genetically distinct and unique. We also wanted to identify those populations which might be of genetic interest, but about which more information was needed.

A series of criteria can be used to evaluate feral populations. The first and easiest is the history of the population. Most populations have been formed through ongoing additions of animals from a variety of breeds or types. These populations can be eliminated from further conservation interest because they are not genetically isolated. Such populations are generally not unique and tend not to be closely adapted to the environment. If lost, they could theoretically be reestablished from founding strains, if this was ever desirable.

Feral populations of interest are those with a history of genetic isolation. This isolation has usually been caused by environmental factors — such as the animals' location on islands, in remote swamps or mountain valleys, or in other relatively inaccessible places — which have discouraged, limited, or prevented subsequent introductions after the founding population became established.

If the history of a population indicates isolation, or if the history is unavailable or inconclusive, an evaluation of the phenotype is the next step. If the phenotype is fairly uniform and consistent with the history of the population, then the population should be considered further.

In some instances, a third evaluation step is possible, which is the biochemical and antigenic investigation of blood types. This step can confirm genetic isolation, uniqueness, and accuracy of history of founding types. This evaluation is most useful for cattle and horses (the species for which baseline data are available) and of less use for swine, sheep, and goats.

Conservation Priority Feral Populations

Burros

Burros have had great success in establishing feral populations in the dry areas of the Southwest. Feral burros vary somewhat from short, pack type to taller, rangy riding type. More research on the feral burro, particularly on its genetic adaptations, is needed.

Cattle

It is quite possible that unique feral strains of cattle of Spanish origin remain in the Southeast, likely found in impenetrable swamps, such as the Okefenokee. Such populations are very difficult to study or even to census. Geographical isolation acts to minimize the threat of crossbreeding or extermination, but also assures that many interesting questions go unanswered.

A very small population of unique feral cattle may persist on Hawaii. This population was also originally Spanish, but may have been crossbred with other domestic cattle, including some Texas Longhorns. It is doubtful that any pure old Hawaiian cattle exist, but it is a high priority to determine if they do.

Goats

The feral goats on the mainland of North America tend to be rather mixed, generic sorts of goats. Few if any feral populations have histories which denote genetic isolation. Goats form feral populations easily, and mainland populations are usually repeatedly contaminated by periodic introductions of domesticated goats, usually dairy breeds.

In contrast are feral goats on islands, particularly in the Caribbean, off the coast of California, and in Hawaii. All of these feral populations are Spanish in origin, but have long ago diverged from the goats of Spain (and each other) and are therefore of genetic significance. The Mona Island and Desecheo Island goats of Puerto Rico are particularly isolated.

The conservation of these populations is difficult, since island goats themselves are usually endangering other unique island lifeforms. For that reason, goats have already been removed from San Clemente and are slated for removal from Santa Catalina Island. Effective populations of these animals need to be established on the mainland, and the collection of semen from island-caught bucks and first-generation bucks on the mainland should be undertaken. These preserved gametes will assure that at least some of the original genetics will be saved.

The feral goats of Saturna Island off of Vancouver, British Columbia, may also be of interest. These animals are phenotypically of the Old English type, unusual in North America, and would represent a geographical adaptation that is also unusual, since this is a northern maritime climate not usually associated with goats.

Horses

Horses have had great success in establishing feral populations. Unlike other feral livestock, they have existed over a wide territory in such numbers that they are a symbol of the American West. While originally Spanish stock, wild horse populations incorporated many waves of introductions, particularly of draft and riding stock designed to increase their size and make them more valuable once caught. As a result, only a very few populations of pure Spanish wild horses remain on the range.

One of the Spanish herds that persists is the Cerbat Mountain/ Marble Canyon herd in western Arizona. These horses are remarkable in being fairly uniform roan of varying shades. The minimal color and blood type variation suggests a small founding population. Many of the Cerbat horses have a lateral gait typical of Spanish strains and distinct from the usual trot. The Cerbat herd is being conserved both on and off the range.

Another strain of Spanish feral horses is represented in the Kiger area of Oregon. These horses are managed by the Bureau of Land Management, which is selecting them for dun color and Spanish type as a way to maintain their distinctiveness, and hence sale value. A breed association has been formed to promote the Kiger Mustang.

The Pryor Mountain horses in Wyoming are also of Spanish type, as confirmed by bloodtyping studies. Programs to assure continuation of this strain as an uncontaminated resource are now underway, as is a breeders' organization for horses adopted from this herd.

Other Spanish strains may occur in isolated areas of Nevada or Utah. It should be possible to document these herds through history and bloodtyping. The ALBC is encouraging the BLM to locate and document any remaining Spanish horses under its management.

Sable Island horses are the only non-Spanish feral horses in North America. The horses range on Sable Island, a long sand bar near the edge of the continental shelf off the east coast of Nova Scotia. The horses are protected by the Canadian government to the extent that absolutely no handling or interference is allowed. This precludes bloodtyping or other invasive studies. The horses are of great theoretical interest since they probably originated from a relatively undifferentiated cold blood type of horse, long since eliminated in Europe.

Sheep

Sheep have had little success in establishing feral populations. Since they are rare, each feral sheep population is of potential genetic interest to ALBC. The three primary feral sheep populations are those of Hog Island, Virginia; Santa Cruz Island, California; and the Hawaiian Islands.

Hog Island sheep originated form several old British types and have become well adapted to low-lying humid environments. Sheep are no longer found on the island itself. Most of the remnants of this tiny breed population are in domestic herds in Virginia, where they are of primary interest to historic sites which can use them to interpret sheep of the 1700s.

Santa Cruz Island sheep are of Spanish Merino origin, likely dating to the early 1800s. Some introductions have been made, but the sheep are still quite unusual, with such relict features as a rat tail and extremely fine fleece. Almost all of the sheep have been extirpated from the island for environmental reasons, but a mainland herd of about 200 has insured the continuation of the breed. Semen has been collected on most of the island-caught and first-generation rams on the mainland.

Hawaiian sheep are not well documented or described. Neither origins nor current population numbers are clear. Sheep are maintained as a game animal on Hawaii, but Mouflons are the most desirable game species, and these have likely replaced feral sheep in most locations. An evaluation of Hawaiian sheep is a high priority.

---

[1]T. L. McKnight, "Feral Livestock in Anglo-America", *University of California Publications in Geography* 16, 1964.

Census Survey Respondents

(Surveys were numbered chronologically by date of contact. Repeated names of respondents indicate additional survey or telephone interviews.)

United States

Alabama:
AL1 - L. D. Hendrick, Jack Reichert, United States Forest Service, Montgomery, AL
AL2 - Kyle G. Crider, The Alabama Conservancy, Birmingham, AL
AL3 - Keith Guise, Wildlife Section, Alabama Fish and Game, Montgomery, AL
AL4 - Skip Bartow, Dale Coleman, Auburn University, Auburn, AL
AL5 - Troy Patterson, Auburn University, Auburn, AL
AL6 - Jo Anne Arthur, Cooperative Extension, Clarke County, AL
AL7 - Tommy Fuller, Cooperative Extension, Washington County, AL
AL8 - Frank Randle, Alabama Sheep and Wool Growers Association, Auburn, AL
AL9 - Gwen Davis, Animal Science/Extension, Tuskegee Institute, Tuskegee, AL
AL10 - LeRoy Simmons, long-time sheep farmer, Falkville, AL

Alaska:
AK1 - Garvan P. Bucaria, Wildlife Biologist, Chugach National Forest, Anchorage, AK
AK2 - Denali National Park, AK
AK3 - Bud Rice, Kenai Fjords National Park, Seward, AK
AK4 - Walter Stieglitz, United States Fish and Wildlife Service, Anchorage, AK
AK5 - Donald E. McKnight, Alaska Department of Fish and Game, Juneau, AK
AK6 - United States Fish and Wildlife Service, Anchorage, AK
AK7 - Ted Huer, United States Fish and Wildlife Service, Homer, AK
AK8 - Mike Blunden, Alaska Maritine National Wildlife Refuge, Homer, AK
AK9 - Denny Zwiefelahofer, Kodiak National Wildlife Refuge, Kodiak, AK

Arkansas:
AR1 - Robert C. McDaniel, Animal and Poultry Science Extension, University of Arkansas, Little Rock, AR
AR2 - John Robinette, Felseuthal National Wildlife Refuge, Crossett, AR
AR3 - Robert L. Mitchell, Ouachita National Forest, Hot Springs, AR

Arizona:
AZ1 - Edward Gastellum, Superintendent, Petrified Forest National Park, AZ
AZ2 - Cabeza Prieta National Wildlife Refuge, Ajo, AZ
AZ3 - Cabeza Prieta National Wildlife Refuge, Ajo, AZ
AZ4 - Raymond L. Evans, USDA, Aphis, Yuma, AZ
AZ5 - Pat Hanrahan, Forest Supervisor, Apache-Sitgreaves National Forest, Springville, AZ
AZ6 - Pat Hanrahan, Forest Supervisor, Apache-Sitgreaves National Forest, Springville, AZ
AZ7 - Raymond L. Evans, USDA, Aphis, Yuma, AZ

AZ8 - Richard W. Marks, Superintendent, Grand Canyon National Park, Grand Canyon, AZ
AZ9 - Imperial National Wildlife Refuge, Martinez Lake, AZ
AZ10 - Raymond Lee, Arizona Fish and Game Department, Phoenix, AZ
AZ11 - John Ray, Grand Canyon National Park, Grand Canyon, AZ
AZ12 - Cabeza Prieta National Wildlife Refuge, Ajo, AZ
AZ13 - Mark Vaniman, Imperial National Wildlife Refuge, Martinez Lake, AZ
AZ14 - Paul Krausman, Wildlife Ecology, University of Arizona, Tuscon, AZ
AZ15 - Kofa National Wildlife Refuge, Kofa, AZ
AZ16 - Russell Orr, Tonto National Forest, Phoeniz, AZ
AZ17 - Barry Braley, Arizona Strip District of the Bureau of Land Management, St George, UT
AZ18 - Larry Allen, Coronado National Forest, Tucson, AZ
AZ19 - Richard W. Marks, Superintendent, Grand Canyon National Park, Grand Canyon, AZ
California:
CA1 - Molly Fuller, Eldorado National Forest, Placerville, CA
CA2 - Tahoe National Forest, Nevada City, CA
CA3 - Dick Riegalhuth, Resources Management, Yosemite National Park, Yosemite, CA
CA4 - Richard F. Johnson, Bureau of Land Management, California State Office, Sacramento, CA
CA5 - Inyo National Forest, Bishop, CA
CA6 - Steven D. Kovach, Natural Resources Management Branch, Western Division, Naval
     Facilities Engineering Command, San Bruno, CA
CA7 - Havasu National Wildlife Refuge, Needles, CA
CA8 - Robert Meron, Klamath National Forest, Yreka, CA
CA9 - Goosenest Ranger District, Klamath National Forest, Macdoel, CA
CA10 - Bill Britton, Modoc National Forest, Alturas, CA
CA11 - Bill Britton, Modoc National Forest, Alturas, CA
CA12 - Dirk Van Vuren, Department of Systematics and Ecology, University of Kansas,
      Lawrence, KS
CA13 - Van Vuren (as above)
CA14 - Van Vuren (as above)
CA15 - Van Vuren (as above)
CA16 - Bruce Coblenz, Department of Fisheries and Wildlife, Oregon State University
      Corvallis, OR
CA17 - Tim Curin, Resources Management, Death Valley National Monument, Death Valley, CA
CA18 - Mark Jorgensen, Anza Borrego Desert State Park, Borrego Springs, CA
CA19 - Al Dennistow, Lassen Volcano National Park, Mineral, CA
CA20 - Gary Davis, Channel Island National Park, Ventura, CA
CA21 - Douglas Propst, Catalina Conservancy, Ventura, CA
CA22 - Terru Russi, Bureau of Land Management, Bishop, CA
CA23 - Frank Ugolini, Resource Management Division, Channel Islands National Park,
      Ventura, CA
Colorado:
CO1 - Dennis G. Lowry, Arapaho and Roosevelt National Forests, Fort Collins, CO
CO2 - Paul Senteney, Grand Mesa, Uncompahgre, Gunnison National Forests, Delta, CO
CO3 - Jack Weissling, Pike and San Gabel National Forests, Pueblo, CO
CO4 - David W. Cook, Wildlife Biologist, San Juan National Forest, Durango, CO
CO5 - David R. Stevens, Rocky Mountain National Park, Estes Park, CO
CO6 - Marilyn Colyer, Mesa Verde National Park, Mesa Verde, CO
Connecticut:
CT1 - George Brys, Department of Environmental Protection, Wildlife Bureau, Hartford, CT
Florida:
FL1 - William C. Bodie, Florida National Forests, Tallahassee, FL
FL2 - Tim Olson, Department of Animal Science, University of Florida, Gainesville, FL
FL1 - Claude H. McGowan, Animal Science Extension, Florida A and M, Tallahassee, FL
Georgia:
GA1 - Jeff Jackson, Cooperative Extension Service, Athens, GA
GA2 - Jim Burkhart, Okefenokee National Wildlife Refuges, Folkston, GA

GA3 - Officer Widener, Lake Lanier State Park, GA
GA4 - Mr. King, Game Warden, Fort Stewart Military Reserve, GA
GA5 - Cumberland Island National Seashore, St. Mary's, GA
GA6 - Susan Bratton, Institute of Ecology, University of Georgia, Athens, GA
Hawaii:
HI1 - David B. Ames, Superintendent, Hawaii Volcanoes National Park, HI
HI2 - Dan Taylor, Resource Management, Hawaii Volcanos National Park, HI
HI3 - Tod M. Lum, Hawaii Department of Land and Natural Resources, Honolulu, HI
HI4 - Jon Giffin, Hawaii Department of Land and Natural Resources, Kamuela, HI
HI5 - Jon Giffin, Hawaii Department of Land and Natural Resources, Kamuela, HI
HI6 - Thomas C. Telfer, Hawaii Department of Land and Natural Resources, Kauai, HI
HI7 - Dan Taylor, Chief of Resources Management, Hawaiian Volcanos National Park, HI
HI8 - Charles Stone, Research Scientist, Hawaii Volcanoes National Park, Hawaii, HI
HI9 - Ron Walker, Chief Wildlife Biologist, Hawaii Department of Land and Natural Resources,
    Honolulu, HI
Idaho:
ID1 - Harry Guenther, USDA Extension Service, Boise, ID
ID2 - Lewis Nelson, Jr, Department of Fish and Wildlife, University of Idaho, Moscow, ID
ID3 - Peter Smith, Range and Wildlife Staff, Salmon River Ranger District, White Bird, ID
ID4 - Sawtooth National Forest, Twin Falls, ID
ID5 - Targhee National Forest, St. Anthony, ID
ID6 - Idaho Wildlife Federation, Pocatello, ID
ID7 - Harold Sherrets, Bureau of Land Management, Boise, ID
ID8 - Robert H. Hale, Bureau of Land Management, Salmon, ID
ID9 - Gene Decker, Bureau of Land Management, Boise, ID
Illinois:
IL1 - Mike Carter, Illinois Department of Natural Resources, Wildlife Division, Springfield, IL
Indiana:
IN1 - John Olson, Department of Natural Resources, Division of Fish and Wildlife,
    Indianapolis, IN
IN2 - Herbert C. Krauch, School of Agriculture, Department of Forestry and Natural Resources,
    Purdue University, West Lafayette, IN
IN3 - Harmone P. Weeks, School of Agriculture, Department of Forestry and Natural Resources,
    Purdue University, West Lafayette, IN
Iowa:
IA1 - Terry Little, Iowa Department of Natural Resources, Des Moines, IA
IA2 - Don Cummings, Wildlife Supervisor, Iowa Department of Natural Resources,
    Des Moines, IA
Kansas:
KS1 - Kansas Fish and Game Commision, Pratt, KS
Kentucky:
KY1 - Lauren Schaaf, Department of Fish and Wildlife Resources, Frankfort, KY
KY2 - Phillip Veluzist, Mammoth Cave National Park, KY
KY3 - Hunting and Fishing Department, Fort Knox Reservation, Fort Knox, KY
Louisiana:
LA1 - Joe Hogan, Kisatchie National Forest, Pineville, LA
LA2 - Tom Edwards, Louisiana Department of Wildlife and Fisheries, Baton Rouge, LA
LA3 - Kerney J. Sonnier, Louisiana Department of Wildlife and Fisheries, Opelousas, LA
LA4 - Kerney J. Sonnier, Louisiana Department of Wildlife and Fisheries, Opelousas, LA
LA5 - Kerney J. Sonnier, Louisiana Department of Wildlife and Fisheries, Opelousas, LA
LA6 - Don Frankey, Animal Science Department, Louisiana State University,
    Baton Rouge, LA
Maryland:
MD1 - Earl H. Hodil, Maryland Wildlife Management, Annapolis, MD
MD2 - R. Bruce Rodgers, National Park Serivce, Berlin, MD
MD3 - Ronald R. Keiper, Department of Biology, Pennsylvania State University,
    Monto Alto, PA

MD4 - Gordon Olson, Resource Manager, Assateague State Park, MD
Massachusetts:
MA1 - Thomas W. French, Director of Natural Heritage and Endangered Species, Massachusetts Division of Fisheries and Wildlife, Boston, MA
Michigan:
MI1 - Richard Elden, Wildlife Division, Michigan Department of Natural Resources, Lansing, MI
Mississippi:
MS1 - Ellen Goetz, Fisheries, Wildlife, and Range, National Forests in Mississippi, Jackson, MS
MS2 - Department of Wildlife Conservation, Jackson, MS
MS3 - Seth Mott, Jackson, MS
MS4 - Don Lewis, Mississippi Department of Wildlife Conservation, Jackson, MS
Missouri:
MO1 - Ray Evans, Missouri Department of Conservation, Jefferson City, MO
MO2 - Ray Evans, Missouri Department of Conservation, Jefferson City, MO
Montana:
MT1 - John Ormiston, Bitterroot National Forest, Hamilton, MT
MT2 - Helena National Forest, Helena, MT
MT3 - Lewis and Clark National Forest, Great Falls, MT
MT4 - James R. Fishburn, Custer National Forest, Billings, MT
Nebraska:
NE1 - Norm Dey, Nebraska Game and Parks Commission, Lincoln, NE
Nevada:
NV1 - Pyramid Indian Tribal Council, Nixon, NV
New Jersey:
NJ1 - New Jersey Division of Fish, Game and Wildlife, Trenton, NJ
New York:
NY1 - Gary Parsons, Department of Environmental Conservation, Albany, NY
NY2 - Sam Moen, Department of Natural Resources, Cornell University, Ithaca, NY
New Mexico:
NM1 - Las Vegas National Wildlife Refuge, Las Vegas, NM
NM2 - Sevilleta National Wildlife Refuge, San Acacia, NM
NM3 - Robert Alexander, Area Manager, White Sands Resource Area, Las Cruces, NM
NM4 - Robert Alexander, Area Manager, White Sands Resource Area, Las Cruces, NM
NM5 - Robert Alexander, Area Manager, White Sands Resource Area, Las Cruces, NM
NM6 - James R. Abbott, Lincoln National Forest, Alamogordo, NM
NM7 - James R. Abbott, Lincoln National Forest, Alamogordo, NM
NM8 - Volney W. Howard Jr, Department of Fishery and Wildlife Sciences, New Mexico State University, Las Cruces, NM
NM9 - Bruce L Morrison, New Mexico Department of Game and Fish, Santa Fe, NM
NM10 - Robert Alexander, Area Manager, White Sands Resource Area, Las Cruces, NM
NM12 - Santa Fe National Forest, Santa Fe, NM
NM13 - Jerry Elson, Santa Fe National Forest, Santa Fe, NM
NM14 - Carson National Forest, Taos, NM
NM15 - Philip R. Settles, Carson National Forest, Blanco, NM NM16; Jerry Elson, Santa Fe National Forest, Santa Fe, NM NM17; Roy Carson, Cibola National Forest, Albuquerque, NM
North Carolina:
NC1 - Back Bay National Wildlife Refuge, Virginia Beach, VA
NC2 - Currituck National Wildlife Refuge, Manteo, NC
NC3 - John Taylor, Alligator River National Wildlife Refuge, Manteo, NC
NC4 - Kent Turner, Cape Hatteras National Seashore, Manteo, NC
North Dakota:
ND1 - Theodore Roosevelt National Park, Medora, ND
ND3 - Theodore Roosevelt National Park, Medora, ND

Ohio:

OH1 - T. A. Bookhout, Ohio Cooperative Fish and Wildlife Research Unit, Ohio State University, Columbus, OH

OH2 - Pat Ruble, Executive Administrator, Wildlife Management and Research, Columbus, OH

Oklahoma:

OK1 - Tishomingo National Wildlife Refuge, Tishomingo, OK

Oregon:

OR1 - Dean Longrie, Mount Hood National Forest, Gresham, OR

OR2 - Siskiyou National Forest, Grants Pass, OR

OR4 - Bob Mountain, Umatilla National Forest, Pendleton, OR

OR5 - Rick Forsman, Powell Butte, OR

OR6 - US Forest Service, Portland, OR

OR7 - Donald Hanson, Malheur National Forest, John Day, OR

OR8 - Malheur National Forest, John Day, OR (followup)

OR9 - Bureau of Land Management, Burns, OR

OR10 - Jim Torland, Oregon Department of Fish and Wildlife, The Dalles, OR

Pennsylvania:

PA1 - Dale E. Sheffer, PA Game Commission, Harrisburg, PA

PA2 - James Bowers, Land Management Officer of the PA Game Commission, Knox, PA

South Carolina:

SC1 - South Carolina Wildlife and Marine Resources Department, Columbia, SC

SC2 - Roger L. Jones, Jr, The South Carolina Nature Conervancy, Columbia, SC

South Dakota:

SD1 - Susan L. Consolo, Badlands National Park, SD

SD2 - Wind Cave National Park, Hot Springs, SD

Tennessee:

TN1 - Tennessee Wildlife Resources Agency, Nashville, TN

Texas:

TX1 - Big Bend National Park, TX

TX2 - Buffalo Lake National Wildlife Refuge, Umbarger, TX

TX3 - David Oates, Texas Parks and Wildlife Department, Lufkin, TX

TX4 - Laguna Atascosa National Wildlife Refuge, Rio Hondo, TX

TX5 - Muleshoe National Wildlife Refuge, Umbarger, TX

TX6 - Gary Waggerman, Texas Parks and Wildlife Department, Edinburg, TX

TX7 - J. D. Murphree Wildlife Management Area, Port Arthur, TX

TX8 - Mike Krueger, Texas Parks and Wildlife Department, Lufkin, TX

TX9 - John D. Wallace, Texas Parks and Wildlife Department, Tyler, TX

TX10 - Steve Demarais, Range and Wildlife Management, Texas Tech Univeristy, Lubbock, TX

Utah:

UT1 - Bryce Canyon National Park, Bryce Canyon, UT

UT2 - Fishlake National Forest, Richfield, UT

UT3 - Zion National Park, Springdale, UT

UT4 - Larry O. Maxfield, Bureau of Land Management, Salt Lake City, UT

UT5 - John Swapp, Bureau of Land Management, Cedar City, UT

UT6 - Dixie National Forest, Cedar City, UT

UT7 - Lyle McNeal, Department of Animal, Dairy, and Veterinary Sciences, Utah State University, Logan, UT

UT8 - Steve Petersburg, Dinosuar National Monument, Dinosaur, UT

UT9 - Barry Braley, Burea of Land Management, St George's, UT

UT10 - Larry Thomas, Canyonlands National Park, Moab, UT

UT11 - Greg Dawson, Bureau of Land Management, Moab, UT

UT12 - Jimmy Forest, Manti-La Sale National Forest, Price, UT

Vermont:

VT1 - Ben Day, Director of Wildlife, Vermont Fish and Wildlife Department, Waterbury, VT

Virginia:
VA1 - Shenandoah National Park, Luray, VA
VA2 - Dennis Holland, Refuge Manager, Chincoteague National Wildlife Refuge, Chincoteague Island, VA
VA3 - Floyd Williams, Ralph Keel, Dismal Swamp National Wildlife Refuge, Suffolk VA
VA4 - Robert Wilson, Chincoteague Island National Wildlife Refuge, Chincogteague, VA
VA5 - Barry Truitt, Virginia Coastal Reserve, The Nature Conservancy, Arlington, VA
Washington:
WA1 - John Hook, Okanogan National Forest, Okanogan, WA
WA1 - Mark J. Madrid, Olympic National Forest, Olympic, WA
WA3 - Robert Chandler, Superintendent, Olympic National Forest, Port Angeles, WA
West Virginia:
WV1 - Edwin D Michael, West Virginia Division of Forestry, Morgantown, WV
WV2 - John Hazel, Monogehela National Forest, Parsons, WV
WV3 - Robert Radtke, US Forest Service, Milwaukee, WI
WV4 - Arnold F. Schulz, Monogehala National Forest, Elkins, WV
WV5 - Rodney Bartgis, Hedgesville, WV
WV6 - Rodney Bartgis, Hedgesville, WV
WV7 - Gary Strawn, West Virginia Department of Natural Resources, Romney, WV
WV8 - Arnold Schultz, Monogehela National Forest, Elkins, WV (followup)
WV9 - James Grafon, US Forest Service (retired), Hambleton, WV
WV10 - Jeff Larson, US Forest Service, Marlington, WV
WV11 - Edwin D. Michael, West Virginia Division of Forestry, Morgantown, WV
WV12 - Jim Crum, Green Briar State Park, MD
WV13 - Ed McGuire, West Virginia Nature Conservancy, Charleston, WV
WV14 - Tom Dotson, West Virginia Department of Natural Resources, Charleston, WV
WV15 - Kenny Painter, Law Enforcement Officer, West Virginia Department of Natural Resources, Charleston, WV
WV16 - Howard Shriver, West Virginia University Agricultural Extension, Morgantown, WV
Wisconsin:
WI1 - Terry Amundson, Wisconsin Department of Natural Resources, Madison, WI
WI2 - Scott Craven, Department of Wildlife Ecology, University of Wisconsin, Madison, WI
Wyoming:
WY1 - Wyoming Game and Fish Department, Cheyenne, WY
WY2 - Rex Corsi, Chief Game Warden, Game and Fish Department, Cheyenne, WY
WY3 - Terry McCreary, Yellowstone National Park, Yellowstone, WY
WY4 - Hillary A. Oden, State Director for Wyoming, Bureau of Land Management, Cheyenne, WY
WY5 - Michael A. Smith, Rnage Management Department, Laramie, WY
WY6 - R. H. Denniston, Laramie, WY
WY7 - Leroy Smalley, Bureau of Land Management, Rawlins, WY
WY8 - John F. Winnepennicky, Bureau of Land Management, Milwaukee, WI
Puerto Rico:
PR1 - Puerto Rico Conservation Trust, San Juan, PR
PR2 - Bernie Rios, Caribbean National Forest, Rio Piedros, PR
PR3 - Caribbean Islands National Wildlife Refuge, Boqueron, PR
PR4 - Roger Di Rosa, US Fish and Wildlife Service, Boqueron, PR
Virgin Islands:
VI1 - Walter I. Knausenberger, University of Virgin Islands, Cooperative Extension Service, St. Croix, VI
VI2 - John Miller, Resources Management, Virgin Islands National Park, St. Thomas, VI
VI3 - L. R. Gulth, Virgin Islands National Park, St. Thomas, VI

174

Canada

Alberta:
AB1 - Vivian Pharis, Cochrana, AB
AB2 - Eldon H Brunns, Alberta Fish and Wildlife Division, Rocky Mountain House, AB
AB3 - D. H. Fregren, Director, Forest Use Branch, Alberta Forest Service, Edmonton, AB
British Columbia:
BC1 - D. R. Halladay, Wildlife Branch, Ministry of Environment and Parks, Victoria, BC
BC2 - R. B. Addison, Range Management, Ministry of Forests, Victoria, BC
BC3 - Valerius Geist, Faculty of Environmental Design, University of Calgary, Calgary, AB
BC4 - R. D. Crawford, Department of Animal Science, University of Saskatchewan
     Saskatoon, SK
New Brunswick:
NB1 - Franklin R. Johnson, Animal Industry Branch, Department of Agriculture,
     Fredrickton, NB
Newfoundland and Labrador:
NF1 - A. O. MacPhee, Chief Wildlife Protection Officer, Department of Culture, Recreation,
     and Youth, Pleasantville, NF
Nova Scotia:
NS1 - Zoe Lucas, Research Scientist, Sable Island Horse Committee, Halifax, NS
Ontario:
ON1 - D. M. Lavigne, Department of Zoology, University of Guelph, Guelph, ON
ON2 - T. I. Hughes, President, Ontario Humane Society, Newmarket, ON
Prince Edward Island:
PEI1 - Fish and Wildlife Division, Department of Community and Cultural Affairs,
     Charlottetown, PEI
Quebec:
QB1 - Rodrigue Bouchard, Ministere du Loisir, de la Chasse, et de la Peche, Quebec, PQ
QB2 - Jean Cinq-Mars, Director, Quebec Region, Canadaian Wildlife Service, Quebec, PQ
Saskatchewan:
SA1 - Bob Oliver, Saskatchewan Parks, Recreation, and Culture, Regina, SK
SA2 - Randolph J. Seguin, Meadow Lake Region, Saskatchewan Parks, Recreation, and Culture,
     Meadow Lake, SK

Glossary

Biodiversity – the variety of habitats, species, and genes which allows adaptation and evolution of biological systems to continue.

Breed – a population of domestic animals in which the individuals vary within defined phenotypic and genotypic parameters. When mated among themselves, the offspring are of this defined type.

Breed association – a group of breeders and other people with an affinity for a particular livestock breed. Activities of an association generally include operation of a registry, development of policies for registration, and breed promotion.

Breed characterization – a documented description of the phenotypic and performance traits of a breed.

Breed registry – a record of individuals which are members of a particular breed. Each individual is assigned a registration number and is identified by its name, date of birth, pedigree, breeder, and owner. Registry records reflect the history of a breed and allow for the tracking of genetic and numeric trends.

Breed-specific products – products which are produced by a particular breed and marketed based on that breed identification. Examples are Certified Angus beef, Churro lamb, and Jacob wool.

Conservation – the intentional protection of something, particularly a natural resource, to prevent exploitation, destruction, or neglect. The term is used in this context to describe living populations of livestock, which continue to evolve within a habitat, while the term "preservation" is applicable to the cryogenic storage of genetic materials, which do not change through time.

Crossbreeding – the mating of individuals of different breeds, usually done to take advantage of hybrid vigor or to obtain offspring with a blend of traits from the parent breeds.

Cryogenic preservation – the freezing and storage of genetic materials, particularly semen and embryos, for use in the future.

Diversified farming – agricultural production involving a mixture of crops and livestock to best utilize available resources.

Ex situ **conservation** – conservation of a breed or population outside of its habitat. This practice is applicable to feral stocks, which may be removed to improve conservation of their habitat. It may also apply to the conservation of livestock outside of agricultural systems, such as at farmparks or zoos.

Extinct – no longer in existence. Livestock breeds may become extinct when the genetic integrity of the breed can no longer be documented, or when the breeding group is so small as to be no longer viable. Breeds may become extinct while the total numbers within a species remain high, but breed extinctions permanently narrow the genetic range of a livestock species.

Feral – a domestic animal or population which has reverted to the wild and is, as a result, under natural rather than human selection. A feral population is a reproducing group of feral animals.

Forage – food for animals which is taken by browsing or grazing. Grass pasture is the most commonly used forage in North America. Forage utilization is the ability of a breed to thrive on a forage diet and may include several elements, including the motivation to graze aggressively and the ability to digest forage efficiently.

Frame – the general conformation and size of an animal, particularly as relevant to carcass size. The term is used primarily to describe cattle, goats, and sheep.

Gene – a unit of the code of inheritance. Implementation of the genetic code is affected by the genes present and the combinations and relationships among them.

Genotype – the defining, heritable code of an individual or a breed which determines its phenotype, behavior, and potential. The genetic consistency of pure breeds is reflected in the consistency of phenotypes.

Genetic diversity – the presence in a breed or population of a large number of genetic variants for each characteristic, allowing for adaptation to changing conditions of selection.

Genetic erosion – the loss of genetic variation within a breed or species.

Genetic uniformity – the presence in a breed or population of a very few genetic variants for each characteristic, often created by strong selection (human or natural) for a particular environment. A uniform population has reduced ability to adapt to changing conditions.

Genus – a category of taxonomic classification between family and species of related plants and animals. The genus name is capitalized as the first word of the scientific name of a species.

Grade – broadly defined as an animal which is not registered. Grade animals may be purebred, crossbred, or of unknown ancestry. Grade animals generally have one registered parent and may be identified by that parentage, for example, as a "grade Holstein."

Herd book – the record of animals registered in a particular breed, usually listed by registration number, pedigree, and date of birth, and appearing in published form. The term "herd book" is generally used for breeds of cattle, goats, and swine; "stud book" for horse breeds; and "flock book" for breeds of sheep.

Hybrid vigor – the performance boost obtained through the crossing of distantly related parents; also called heterosis.

Improvement of breeds – a general term which may include increasingly effective selection for desired traits within a pure breed (characteristic of the livestock industry over the past two centuries) or the introduction of outside blood simply to make the breed "better" in the eyes of breeders. In modern agriculture, improvement has come to mean intensifying and standardizing production characteristics.

Industrial livestock – breeds or stocks which are specialized for rapid, maximum production of a single product (such as meat or milk) when given high levels of inputs (such as feed) and kept in a closely controlled environment. An industrialized production system implies one in which uniform animals are units with predictable performance which can be replaced by other identical individuals when performance declines.

Inputs – foods, housing, medical care, and other provisions given to animals in order to keep them healthy and productive. Low input systems are characterized by the raising of animals out of doors and the use of forage which animals must harvest themselves. High input systems include grain feeds, high energy supplements, growth enhancers, and climate controlled housing, all characteristic of industrialized livestock production and the costs associated with such husbandry practices.

In situ **conservation** – conservation within the native habitat, particularly relevant to the conservation of feral and landrace populations, but also characteristic of conservation within the farming systems and environments where breeds were initially developed.

Landrace – livestock breed or population which has been shaped through natural as well as human selection. Generally, landrace populations have been loosely managed and are not as consistent in appearance as standardized breeds. They tend to retain climate adaptation, fertility, maternal instinct, parasite and disease resistance, and other characteristics associated with natural selection.

Livestock – domestic animals used in agriculture. Globally, a wide range of species are considered livestock, including guinea pigs, camels, elephants, llamas, reindeer, and water buffalo, though the traditional livestock species of North America are asses, cattle, goats, horses, sheep, swine, and poultry.

Oxen – any cattle trained and used for work, most often castrated males.

Phenotype – the appearance of an individual, population, or breed, which is determined by its genotype.

Ruminant – cud-chewing mammals of the suborder *Ruminantia* which have complex four chambered stomachs that enable them to digest rough forage. Ruminants include cattle, goats, sheep, camels, deer, and giraffes.

Selection – the process by which the next generation of a population or breed is chosen. Under natural selection, the most successful individuals produce the most offspring and so contribute the most to the next generation and thus to the future gene pool. Under human selection, breeders select as breeding stock the individuals with the traits they most desire for the next generation.

Soundness – healthy and free from defects, particularly used to describe the feet and legs.

Species – the category of taxonomic classification below the genus to describe animals which possess in common one or more distinctive characters and may interbreed. The species is the second word in the scientific name and is not capitalized.

Strain – a sub-population of a breed that is more closely related than to the breed as a whole. Strains are identifiable elements of a breed's genetic diversity and their conservation is often significant in the conservation of a breed's genetic breadth.

Sustainable agriculture – agricultural practices emphasizing the use of renewable, on-farm resources with the goal of long term management without the continual addition of outside elements. Generally, sustainable agriculture is characterized as lower in inputs and more diversified than are modern industrial systems.

Variety – a group of animals within a breed which have shared morphological traits, such as color or patterns, hair type or presence or absence of horns. A variety may or may not have significant genetic differences (created by genetic drift or selection) from the rest of the breed.

Index

211041